NEW YORK REVIEW BOOKS
POETS

HAYIM NAHMAN BIALIK (1873–1934) is widely considered the greatest Hebrew literary figure of his age. Born in the Ukrainian village of Radi, he was orphaned at the age of seven and sent to live with his pious grandparents. At seventeen he left for the famous Volozhin Yeshiva in Lithuania and then for Odessa, where he emerged as the youngest of a remarkable group of Hebrew writers and intellectuals. He and his wife, Manya, made their home in Odessa for more than twenty years but were forced to flee the newly established Soviet Union in 1921 for Germany. In 1924, he set sail for British Mandatory Palestine. He died in Vienna.

PETER COLE is the author, most recently, of *Draw Me After: Poems*; *That Simple?... and That Complicated: Conversations on Poetry and Translation*; and *Hymns & Qualms: New and Selected Poems and Translations*. His many books of translation include *The Dream of the Poem: Hebrew Poetry from Muslim and Christian Spain, 950–1492* and *The Poetry of Kabbalah*, as well as contemporary poetry and fiction by Aharon Shabtai, Taha Muhammad Ali, Yoel Hoffmann, and others. Cole has received numerous honors, among them an American Academy of Arts and Letters Award, the National Jewish Book Award, the PEN Translation Prize, and a MacArthur Fellowship.

P.P. 3/3

Hayim Nahman Bialik

On the Slaughter

SELECTED AND TRANSLATED BY PETER COLE

NYRB/POETS

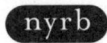 NEW YORK REVIEW BOOKS *New York*

THIS IS A NEW YORK REVIEW BOOK
PUBLISHED BY THE NEW YORK REVIEW OF BOOKS
207 East 32nd Street, New York, NY 10016
www.nyrb.com

Portions of this book first appeared in *The Poetry of Kabbalah: Mystical Verse from the Jewish Tradition* (Yale University Press, 2015). Earlier versions of "Bring Me in Under Your Wing" and "On the Slaughter" first appeared in *The Paris Review* and *The Yale Review*.

Frontispiece: Moshe Gershuni, *On the Slaughter* (1988), courtesy of the Jerusalem Print Workshop.

Library of Congress Cataloging in Publication Control Number: 2025024916

ISBN 979-8-89623-001-4
Available as an electronic book; ISBN 979-8-89623-002-1

Cover and book design by Emily Singer

The authorized representative in the EU for product safety and compliance is eucomply OÜ, Pärnu mnt 139b-14, 11317 Tallinn, Estonia, hello@eucompliancepartner.com, +33 757690241.

Printed in the United States of America on acid-free paper.
10 9 8 7 6 5 4 3 2 1

Contents

"Texts that are inertly of their time stay there: those which brush up unstintingly against historical constraints are the ones we keep with us, generation after generation."

—EDWARD SAID

I

POLITICAL POEMS lead strange lives. More often than not they die on the vine of events they spring from. Contexts fade, and—high historical stakes notwithstanding—the whole enterprise can come to seem pointless, a far cry from Ezra Pound's definition of literature as news that stays news. Which is why we hear again and again that poetry and politics just don't mix.

Though, of course, they do. Sometimes violently.

Hayim Nahman Bialik's 1903 open wound of a Hebrew poem, "On the Slaughter," is a case in point: "Skies," it begins, "have mercy..." This dark lyric constituted Bialik's immediate response to an attack that year on the Jewish community in Kishinev, the backwater capital of Bessarabia (now Moldova's Chişinău), as Passover and Easter celebrations began to wind down. After a week of intermittent rain and the usual seasonal warnings about impending troubles, on the afternoon, evening, and night of April 19, and through the following day, a medley of ax-, pick-, knife-, and club-wielding seminarians, peasants, workers, and students descended on Jewish homes at the city's center and then headed for poorer Jewish neighborhoods on the muddy slopes of town. Incited by a local newspaper's anti-Semitic articles and rumors that Jews had ritually murdered Christian children in order to supply blood for their Passover matzo, vodka-fueled mobs hacked and cudgeled to death forty-nine Jews, or drowned them in outhouse feces; they wounded hundreds; raped women and girls repeatedly; and looted over a thousand homes and shops. (A few months later—in another right-wing daily he edited—the publisher and editor of that paper printed a serialized version of what would come to be known as *The Protocols of the Elders of Zion*.)

The world press covered the Kishinev massacre widely, as new technologies made possible the immediate distribution of dramatic photographs of the dead. While subsequent attacks on Jewish communities during the Bolshevik Revolution were far more devastating—resulting in between 50,000–200,000 deaths—it is, arguably, Kishinev that opened the way into English for the hitherto obscure Russian word meaning "riot" or "wreaking havoc": *pogrom*, etymologically a *thundering through*.

The thirty-year-old Bialik was at that point living some 120 miles southeast of Kishinev, in the balmier and more cosmopolitan Black Sea port city of Odessa. He'd published his first book of poems two years earlier to serious acclaim in highbrow Hebrew circles, and the rising literary star was immediately asked by an Odessan Jewish commission to head an investigative delegation and document the devastation in Kishinev. Bialik and his small group of fact finders spent some five weeks in the city, taking photographs, assembling documents and statistics, and interviewing victims at length, mostly in Yiddish, then translating these interviews into Hebrew. With his extraordinary patience and gifts for eliciting detailed, candid narratives, the young poet made a striking impression on the locals. "Even the most reluctant who had blocked out their traumas unburdened themselves before him," recounted one local observer. "[They] spoke to him in their everyday language, directly from the heart, about events that they blocked from consciousness and buried deep inside. His approach inspired their confidence and helped them to overcome shame. He approached them with genuine warmth, tenderness, acceptance, and good judgment."

Having gathered his grotesque testimony and soaked himself in the landscape and aura of the carnage, Bialik retreated to his father-in-law's summer house between his childhood home of Zhitomir and the regional capital, Kiev, ostensibly to pull together his two hundred pages of handwritten notes and write his report. What happened next remains mysterious. Instead of composing an official account for the commission, Bialik set to work on what would emerge as a 272-line poem about the butchery, narrated by an impoverished, fallen, and baffled deity who directs a prophet-like poet-witness through the killing fields and a reenvisioning of the assault:

Get up and go to the city of slaughter and come to
    the yards
and see with your own eyes and run your hands
    along the fences
and trees and stones, and across the walls' plaster,
    and touch
the dried blood and stiffened tissue spilled from
    skulls of the fallen ...

This caustic voice brought down from on high by the horror excoriates the shattered Jewish community, exposing its suffering but also its spiritual desiccation and essential passivity.

And they made my glory great in the world and
    sanctified my name,
fleeing like mice in flight, concealing themselves
    like fleas,
they died the death of dogs, there where they were
    found...

Bialik finished the poem toward the end of the summer. "The day on which this great poem was written," averred the poet's younger Bessarabian writer and friend Yaakov Fichmann, "may be the most important date in the history of modern Hebrew poetry." The report for the commission was never submitted.

For two decades or so prior to the 1903 pogrom, scores of Hebrew and Yiddish poems had been written about attacks on the Jewish communities in the Pale of Settlement, almost all of them predictable and sentimental. Bialik's work, says literary historian Alan Mintz, was the exception. "'City of Slaughter,'" he writes, "is astonishing, austere, and path-breaking." It is also, he noted, "founded on a lie." The "lie" Mintz refers to concerns the fact that the testimony collected by Bialik (and published only in 1991) shows clearly that Kishinev's Jewish community wasn't nearly as passive as the poet depicts it—that there *had* been attempts at self-defense. And yet, Bialik chose not to include the evidence of this in his poem, most likely because he wanted the work to rouse rather than console and to serve the greater cause of Jewish awakening—which meant, above all, the revival of Hebrew and the reimagining of a viable and vital Jewish life in the present.

Whatever he was thinking or feeling, the poem ends up turning on the victims. The revered popular fiction writer and friend of the poet Mendele Mocher Seforim (S. Y. Abramovitsh) likened it to "a second pogrom," saying: "Nu, Bialik!... When he writes a poem...he always says something that is entirely his. Still, I can't forgive him for the Kishinev matter.... Just imagine, would you, that wild beasts, the worst scum of the human race, were to attack me and my wife and my children, were to murder and kill and carry out every kind of abomination, were to afflict me with every kind of torture—and along comes someone like some preacher who moralizes at me and throws salt on my wounds...as though the people itself were guilty." He wasn't alone in his dismay. Kafka, who read the poem in Bialik's own loose Yiddish translation and heard a 1911 lecture about it in Prague, was also put off at what he saw as the poet's exploitation of the victims. And yet, there is much more to this Jeremiad than an indictment of the pathetic detachment and venality of Eastern European Jewry. Instead, the tectonic upheaval of the poem brings us into the heart of a people and a poet in crisis.

A work of compounded sympathy and staggering cruelty, "City of Slaughter" confronts its readers with graphic and nearly forensic assessments of the violence and turns the bloody occasion into one of the harshest works in the vast library of Jewish self-castigation. At the same time, it makes palpable the way in which many Jews feel in their bones the long, abattoirish gutters running from Kishinev's anti-Semitic onslaught back to the dirges and elegies for bludgeoned and lost Jewish communities across the centuries. "Bialik's Kishinev poem," writes Mintz, "will not leave us alone."

Make that "Bialik's Kishinev *poems*." Over the past ten years in particular, "On the Slaughter," Bialik's earlier response to the pogrom, has become a rhetorical touchstone in pivotal Israeli responses to Palestinian violence. Israel's prime minister has twice cited two of the poem's three most famous lines in statements to the Israeli public and for a global audience. In June of 2014, three Israeli teenagers were kidnapped while hitchhiking home from their West Bank yeshivas. Coming out of a cabinet meeting convened eighteen days later, just after their corpses were found, Benjamin Netanyahu stood before members of the Hebrew press, expressed his condolences to the families, and declaimed: "Vengeance like this, for the blood of a child, / Satan has yet to devise." Revenge would be coming, he promised, and went on in his own words: "Hamas is responsible—and Hamas will pay." For good measure, the prime minister's office tweeted Bialik's lines as well.

And then it was Saturday, October 7, 2023, a holiday morning, and Hamas's al-Aqsa Flood was pouring across Jewish communities along Israel's border with Gaza. This was *not* a pogrom, as historian Steven Zipperstein has pointed out (the power dynamics differed at root), but the historical near-rhymes, as he notes, disturb nonetheless: some 1,200 people were murdered in a variety of gruesome ways, women were raped and their bodies mutilated, homes were burnt, and roughly 250 people were taken hostage to Gaza. Here too a selective reading of "On the Slaughter" fanned already menacing flames, as once again Netanyahu chimed in, with an official if creaky English-language post at 9:25 that evening: "As Bialik wrote, 'Revenge for the blood of a little child has not yet been devised by Satan.' All of the places which Hamas is deployed, hiding and operating in that wicked city, we will turn them into rubble."

In both cases Netanyahu's citations of Bialik's poem skipped the line that precedes what he sent out to rouse his listeners: "And cursed be he who cries—Revenge!" And in both cases massive Israeli attacks on Gaza followed. The 2014 war claimed the lives of more than 1,300 Palestinians—most of them children—and fifty-nine Israelis, three of them civilians. As I revise these lines in April 2025, the Palestinian death toll in the current Gaza war has exceeded 50,000. Nearly two million people have been displaced (some 80 percent of the Strip's population), in many cases with no homes to return to. Famine is rife, communities have been ravaged, "safe zones" are lethal, and universities, mosques, churches, libraries, and cultural institutions have been obliterated.

And this, too, the strange life of a poem like "On the Slaughter" anticipates: that the slaughtered can become the slaughterers. That if one came across Bialik's poem in its potent 1966 translation into Arabic by the charismatic Rashid Hussein, one of the first stars of modern Palestinian poetry, it would make perfect sense that the poem had found a home in the rhythms and rhymes of Arabic prosody and that it has lived on in the circulatory and respiratory systems of at least some Palestinian readers, through the 1982 Sabra and Shatila massacre in Beirut and into the Gazan present.

Bialik can hardly be considered a pacifist. And his poetry was, as Fichman wrote, "by no means a poetry of appeasement." His political moderation and "neutrality" notwithstanding—he never affiliated himself with any political party—Bialik's "entire being was ready for battle and the agon of struggle, [but he] was nonetheless in his innermost being a constructive person.... All uprooting, every act of destruction—even in the name of correction or repair (tikkun)—was repulsive to him.... The Jewish revolutionary spirit, and especially the reckless foundation of it—which above all destroyed itself—he could see only as a 'Satanic fervor,' and he, a man of passions and fury, the poet of the 'poems of wrath,' recoiled from the abyss of ruin." While the poem and the lines in question are by no means easily reducible to a course of political action, critics and Bialik himself have made it clear that, as the poet Tuvya Rübner has written: "Within the cosmic domain in which the poem operates, revenge—which is a human weakness—can hardly exist."

Though of course the all-too-human *desire* for it can be acknowledged, even as it's rejected. But in the world that produces Kishinev, Bialik seems to be saying, vengeance wouldn't begin to address the injustice that has been unleashed; the only hope, glimpsed in a moment of despair, is that the corrosive blood of the dead might bring about the final collapse of a depraved state of affairs, perhaps with a chance to begin again. To seek vengeance would be to make oneself worse than Satan. And that is precisely how Bialik characterized Jewish militancy in Palestine in the late 1920s and 30s.

2

"A broad face, frank, fair skinned and clear eyed.... There is something rural about him, a man of the earth...though the mouth's outline is exceptionally refined," Fichman wrote. It's "a typical Slavic face etched with perennial Jewish concern. Whenever the joyful surge in the blood asserts itself, so does the sorrow. When he concentrates, his eyes close; but when they open, they reflect a bluish gleam suggestive of the green woods and wide meadows he absorbed in his childhood."

Born in 1873 in one of the forty or so huts comprising the northwestern Ukrainian village of Radi, Bialik spent the first five years of his life on the forest tract managed by his Torah-devoted but distant and detached father of Hasidic stock, Yitzhak Yosef. When his father's timber business failed, the family moved to the outskirts of the nearest and very Jewish city of Zhitomir, where Yitzhak Yosef opened a store and later a tavern. Bialik's mother, the darker and moody Dinah Privah, peddled hand-knitted socks and other goods in the local markets. Both had been married previously, and widowed. Two years after the move, Yitzhak Yosef died, and Bialik's put-upon mother brought him to live with his strict paternal grandparents, who saw to his religious education.

When he was seventeen, Bialik left Zhitomir for the famous Lithuanian yeshiva in Volozhin. Its students, he'd heard, read well beyond the standard religious curriculum, and independent thinking flourished there. During the eighteen months of his study at Volozhin, he made friends, began writing, but eventually grew weary of yeshiva life and, in the first of many restless moves, left for Odessa eager to encounter the city's writers. He stayed for six months, teaching Hebrew privately, reading Dostoevsky and Gogol in the original (his Russian had improved at Volozhin), and being tutored in German. He also submitted some of his poetry to the distinguished editor of a new Hebrew literary journal, *Pardes* (The Orchard). When pressure from the Russian authorities forced the Volozhin Yeshiva to close—they considered it a center of social unrest—Bialik had to return to Zhitomir, as he'd hidden from his grandparents the fact that he had already dropped out.

Shortly after his grandfather died in 1893, the twenty-year-old poet married Manya Averbuch, a local girl he'd been engaged to for less than a year, and went to work with her father in the timber trade in Korostyshev, near Kiev. Most of the week he'd spend alone in the woods, or with his workers, reading into the evenings.

All the while, new poems were coming. His submission

to *Pardes* had been accepted and published in 1892 to considerable praise, alongside work by the leading literary lights of the day, including Shalom Aleichem, Mendele Mocher Seforim, and Y. L. Gordon. Young Bialik's contribution—a poem about a bird—appears toward the end of the volume, sandwiched between a Hebrew translation of a poem about a teardrop by Heine and an essay by Simon Dubnow, the historian who would, among other things, go on to head the Kishinev pogrom commission. The thirty-three-year-old editor of the journal, Yehoshua Ravnitzky, eventually became Bialik's closest friend and partner in an extensive project to gather and publish major Hebrew works of the past and present. Their enterprise unfolded as part of a larger movement of Jewish rebirth, and in the Odessan case its leader was the journal's sponsor (and a regular contributor), Ahad Ha'Am, "One of the People," the pen name of Asher Ginsburg, whose vision of a cultural or spiritual Zionism—as opposed to Herzl's "political Zionism"—Bialik identified with in the deepest way.

His adventure in the timber business, meanwhile, had failed miserably, and impoverishment loomed once again. An invitation to take up a private Hebrew tutoring position in Sosnowiec, Poland (near Krakow), rescued him from the financial brink and from his woodland isolation. In Sosnowiec his poetry thrived, even as he came to despise the materialism of the local Jewish community and its entrenched apathy. He lived there for three years before accepting a better teaching post that allowed him to return to Odessa, which, with Warsaw, had developed into one of the two hubs of the modern Hebrew literary renaissance and become home to an impressive array of Jewish writers, editors, and cultural arbiters.

He and Manya (who never had children) would live in Odessa for almost all of the next twenty years, up through the various stages of the Russian Revolution. The elegant and relatively young seaside city—founded by Catherine the Great in 1794—infused him with new energies: its light and air, and its intellectual company; its large and forward-looking Jewish community (Jews comprised nearly a third of the population); its linguistic, ethnic, and commercial diversity; and, always, the promise of the sea. The historical exigencies of the day also challenged him, and his poetry matured, its music deepening and growing more complex, its scope widening, as in the Kishinev poems. His greatest poetry took shape during these Odessa years.

Apart from a fifteen-month interlude in the still more open and "melodic" Warsaw (as Fichman put it) to take up yet another editorial position, and a three-month trip to then-Ottoman Palestine in 1909, Odessa remained Bialik's home until 1921, when it became clear that Hebrew and Jewish culture would have no future in the Bolshevik society that was taking shape in Russia. Hebrew presses had been banned from publishing, Jewish communal activity was prohibited, and personal survival and safety now felt threatened. Only after extreme and risky efforts in Moscow and through various back channels, including the intervention of Maxim Gorky, did the fifty-year-old Bialik obtain permission to emigrate. On June 21, 1921, with Ravnitzky and the families of ten other Jewish writers, Bialik and Manya gathered at the Odessa port and boarded a ship for Istanbul. From there the others set sail for British Mandatory Palestine, while the Bialiks stayed on in Turkey for several months, planning a trip to Berlin to tend to business of various sorts.

As it happened, Bialik spent a full three years in Berlin and Bad Homburg, where he supervised the publication of his collected works and solidified the European operations of the publishing enterprise he'd undertaken in Odessa with Ravnitzky and intended to continue in Palestine. Finally, in March 1924, via Trieste and Alexandria, Manya and Bialik made their way to Tel Aviv, where the poet received a hero's welcome. There he oversaw the building of a kind of orientalist castle that immediately became known as "Beit Bialik" (Bialik House), wrote almost no poetry (though he continued to issue up his powerful essayistic prose), and soon wearied of the constant fuss and attention and rounds of responsibilities. Although he served as a kind of cultural mayor of the new city and father figure to the Jewish Zionist community in Palestine, he also took every opportunity to travel abroad for business; eventually he rented out the small palace that bore his name and moved to a modest apartment in a nondescript adjacent suburb.

By then he'd been suffering for several years from various ailments, including cherry-sized kidney stones, and he followed his physicians' advice to undergo treatment in Vienna. Specialists there determined that he needed to have his enlarged prostate removed, and in June 1934 surgery was performed, successfully. He'd been convalescing at the hospital for nearly two weeks when, on July 4, while reading the paper, he cried out in Yiddish that his heart was exploding. Death came quickly: a blood-clot embolism had blocked his coronary arteries. He was sixty-one. Arrangements were made to have his body shipped back to Tel Aviv, where his funeral took place, attended by some one hundred thousand people—which is to say, half of the Jewish population of Palestine.

3

Bialik's reputation as the voice of his age and *the* major figure of modern Hebrew poetry rests on a foundation of some thirty poems that sang, cut, felt, sculpted, and blasted their way through the haze of a musty nineteenth-century Hebrew romanticism. A handful of classically buttressed visionary essays draw readers continually as well, along with a small corpus of short fiction, scores of informal talks on wide-ranging topics, and, increasingly as he got older, that ongoing project of cultural retrieval he called *kinus,* or in-gathering—not of exiles and refugees, but of texts in danger of being lost forever to the world of rapidly changing or vanishing Jewishness.

For a variety of social and cultural reasons, Hebrew came late to the party of the modern. Traditional Jewish men of Bialik's day studied, read, and to a certain extent wrote Hebrew in religious contexts from a very young age. But speaking was generally reserved for the vernacular wherever Jews lived—Arabic in the Islamic world; Ladino in the Ottoman Empire; German, Yiddish, Russian, and other languages in the Austro-Hungarian Empire and the Pale of Settlement. Bialik's mother tongue, in other words, wasn't Hebrew—that was the tongue of his fathers. His native language was Yiddish, which he continued to speak to his wife and his friends, even in "the Hebrew city," Tel Aviv. "Yiddish speaks itself," he'd say, "Hebrew has to be spoken." And Gershom Scholem, the great Berlin-born scholar of Kabbalah, tells how when he'd visit Bialik on Friday evenings during the poet's last years in Tel Aviv he'd hear Bialik say to his wife or the other guests in Yiddish, in part to tease him, "*Der yekke* (the German Jew) has come, we've got to speak the Holy Tongue." Which is to say, Hebrew.

At the beginning of the Hebrew twentieth century, direct individual rather than collective expression still constituted the stuff of a cultural revolution and Bialik was its poet. He drew on all the registers of Hebrew literary history—the sublime style of the Bible; the grounded specificity of the Mishna; the dense and dexterous kineticism of the Gemara's disputation and exchange; the narrative and exegetical figuration of rabbinic works and mystical texts; the unrivaled music and emotional range of the great Andalusian Hebrew poetry. And from that miraculous-seeming synthesis he forged a lyric and neo-prophetic idiom that felt at once immediate and resonant, personal and everyone's, *not* the vernacular or at all colloquial, and yet intimate, lit with the charge of Jewish longing and learning and life.

He began composing in a delayed Romantic mode, but one that was soon tempered by his immersion in Symbolist, Decadent, and—above all—high-resolution Russian realist literature. This he grafted onto a trunk of retooled biblical elementalism and, when called for, its brimstone—with a rabbinic steadiness of pitch and tone added for ballast. The voice that came forth feels like a peculiar cross between

Wordsworth, the Psalmist, the major biblical prophets, Lermontov, and Thomas Hardy as the Poet of Cusps. For all of his insular Jewishness and commitment to a future for Jews in the Land of Israel, Bialik started out as, and in many ways remained to the end, a Russian poet with "the energy, the moral sincerity and torment, the chiaroscuro moods, the love of the...landscape and the changing season" that one would expect from a poet in that tradition. Hence at least some of the steep decline in his production as the Russian worlds he knew gave way—and as he himself tried to adjust to the "land of the sun," where the Sephardic system of Hebrew pronunciation prevailed and effectively rendered obsolete the suppler and gentler Yiddish-inflected Ashkenazic prosody of his poems. It is one of the great ironies of Bialik's career that, when at last he found himself in a Hebrew-speaking culture, it turned out to be somehow inimical to the deepest drives of his art.

"You should know that my soul is rooted in the diaspora," he'd written late in 1903 to a colleague who'd repeatedly tried to persuade him to accept a position as a teacher in Palestine at a new school being established for the orphans of Kishinev. "Perhaps the Shekhinah abides with me only in sadness and on defiled soil." Justifications apart, little in the way of song wafted up from him once he settled in Tel Aviv.

Bialik's poetics of belatedness notwithstanding, the sheer force in his poems of his presence and prescience—his blending of lyric and moral leverage; his sensitivity, fearlessness, fury, and vulnerability; his powerfully integrated intellect and his capacious vision of a Jewishness that might evolve through the deepest translation of its endangered materials—all coalesce in his verse to form a poetry of the first intensity. His 1927 essay "On the Sacred and Secular in Language" sheds light on the broader vision that drove him from his late teens on: "There are transmigrations in language: many souls pass through, one after another, each leaving its spirit in the word. All of these spirits cling to the word."

Keeping those souls and spirits alive remained Bialik's abiding aim, whether he was writing poems or essays or stories in Hebrew or Yiddish, teaching children or composing poems for them, editing the finest Hebrew literary journals of his day, publishing volume after volume of classical Hebrew literature through the ages, or inventing words to stoke and extend the language's reach. The core of that ongoing life involved a self-correcting or balancing dynamic that Bialik called *ha-shniyut b'yisrael*, a term that's usually translated as "Jewish dualism." Because of its essentially dialogic and relational nature, however, it might better be thought of as a dialectical coupling: sacred and profane, homeland and diaspora, letter and spirit, shepherd and farmer, Yahweh and Elohim, concretion and abstraction, *halakhah* (the literature of religious law) and *aggadah* (anecdotal wisdom in action), and, as the title of his best-known essay has it, "Revealment and Concealment in Language."

The alternating current between each of these pairings runs, as Bialik felt it, like an incandescent filament through Jewish life and has sustained it through calamity, accomplishment, and the normal mysticism—and tedium—of its dailiness. "*Halakhah* wears a frown," begins another of his still widely cited essays, "*aggadah* a smile. The one is pedantic, severe, unbending—all justice; the other is accommodating, lenient, pliable—all mercy." A talk he gave in Berlin in 1922, during that limbo period between his leaving Odessa and settling in Tel Aviv, addresses this question of duality and sustenance directly: "A people whose fate is determined by only one tendency and which puts all its weight on one foundation must depart from the world stage when this power is no longer strong and its rule has evaporated. A people, however, which is in equal measure under the rule of two forces lives forever."

Bialik's entire body of work—from his poetry to the ancient and medieval literature he sought to bring into a reimagined present throughout his life and for future generations—took shape under the aegis of that doubleness, which might effectively be considered a kind of translation: translation of materials through which, as the novelist José Saramago once put it, something older "has to be transformed...in order to keep on being what it was." In that respect, the fructifying tension between original (which is in many ways already a translation) and translation (which becomes an original) combine to form yet another one of the dyads latent in Bialik's vision.

There is the matter of his own bilingualism, or diglossia, to be sure. But the translational compound at the heart of his enterprise goes further still. It runs through the Yiddish translations of his poetry—made by some of the finest Yiddish writers of the day, and sometimes by Bialik himself. Of particular interest here are the translations of his work into Russian by Vladimir Jabotinsky, who was well into his own transformation from aspiring multilingual poet, novelist, journalist, and bohemian to greater notoriety as a militaristic right-wing nationalist thinker and activist—one whose later Revisionist Zionist ideology Bialik came to consider diabolic. The two would part ways sharply. In another ironic twist, it was Jabotinsky's contemporaneous translation of "City of Slaughter" that helped make Bialik the "national poet" and brought him to widespread recognition beyond Russian Jewry—the world's largest at the time—and out to writers such as Maxim Gorky, Vladimir Mayakovsky, and others. Eight years later Jabotinsky's selection and translation of poems by Bialik sold tens of thousands of copies, which is to say, many more than the poet's work in its original Hebrew. In a review of Jabotinsky's translations, Gorky speaks of Bialik as a great poet of, at once, wrath, grief, despair, and love for the world—"a rare and perfect embodiment of the spirit of his people," a writer whose work transcends the particulars of its circumstances, like that of Isaiah and Job and great lyric poets through the ages.

4

What first drew me into the Bialikian forcefield more than three decades ago had nothing to do with slaughter or modern Hebrew per se. It was the vividness of Bialik's prose about *kinus*, particularly his descriptions of encountering the long-neglected Arabized Andalusian Hebrew poetry of the eleventh and twelfth centuries, the state of which he likened in 1924 to "a desolate plain of dry bones scattered with the stones and shards of a palace in ruin."

"From all the branches of our literature," he wrote, "from

every corner in which a part of the 'holy spirit' of the nation is hidden...we have to extract the best, scattered sparks, to join them together." Over the years I translated a number of his poems that had attached themselves to me for one reason or another. But it came as a complete surprise in the weeks and months after October 7, 2023, that it was Bialik who rose up out of our violent and in many ways desperate moment and spoke to me: Bialik not as the proto-Zionist oracle of vengeance that politicians have concocted, but Bialik as a poet of poise under soul-crushing pressure—a poet far darker than most readers realize, yet one who keeps his eye on the prize that has construction and complex love at its center, albeit a love riddled with ambivalence and laced with an often acerbic critique of himself and his own community, and of his people's tormentors and would-be exterminators.

Here too the strange lives and lure of poems and their politics take hold. Writing in 1685 about translating from a miscellany of major Latin writers, John Dryden noted that things sometimes appear in his English renderings that at first glance might seem to be additions to the text or projections of the translator. And yet, he proposes, they are in fact "secretly in the poet," as though the reagent of translation-plus-time had brought these hidden things out and animated them for the translator and possibly for a new generation of readers. So it is, for instance, in our encounter with Bialik's debut, "To the Bird." As the young-old speaker longs for safety at home and "song" from a far-off land, a shadowy anxiousness asserts itself in ways that likely went unheard in late-nineteenth-century romantic readings of the poem, which wonders "if in the land of the sun as well / there's trouble, or something's gone wrong." Likewise, in the later "Scroll of Fire," the light of Jewish value and valence—Yahweh's glory—vanishes into secret places to preserve itself against catastrophe and ruin. Sometimes, in other words, the radical humaneness of a poet's vision refracted through translation calls itself into fresh and jarring question.

That counter-reading lurking in the poems is what I've listened for as I've made these translations—that less-than-fashionable complexity encoded within the deceptively simple surface of Bialik's verse, its rhythmic suppleness and immediacy, its acoustic cohesion and annealed clarity, all of which abound in lyric masterpieces like "Bring Me in Under Your Wing," "Summer Dies," and "The Pool"; that coexistence of at-homeness and rebellion within tradition, and the way in which the referents of a poem seem always about to unmoor themselves from the narrative line and hover above it, ready to speak to a providential addressee (as Mandelstam put it). Central to that capacity for reception are the pockets of silence that open up in the spaces of the work, in its stanzas, its rooms, its fields.

Reading Bialik today, with cries of revenge in the air and the streets, and bodies piling up on the ground and beneath it, I find myself thinking of the many voices and presences that cling to the letters of his lines. Channeling the music of his mind, the minute particulars of his sensual and intellectual experience, and *something* of the tremors of history that rattled him, I sense him as a poet of endangered doublings, a bard of ambivalence and difficult betweenness, a psalmist of the gap that the events and Jewishness of his day bequeathed to him. And that's what I've found myself wanting to track—that precarity and richness of being between, of living with those uneasy couplings.

The worlds Bialik moved through are gone, but the hard questions he faced—the "historical constraints" he brushed up against and the texts and textures he felt driven to render into new poems—endure with Hardyesque "undervoicings . . . of loss," which themselves accrue as a kind of gain. And which, it seems, is why he stays with us, and, just now, feels eerily closer than ever.

—*Peter Cole*
New Haven,
April 2025

Poems

On the Slaughter

Skies—have mercy.
If you hold a God
(to whom there's a way
that I haven't found), pray for me.
Me, my heart has died.
There is no prayer on my lips.
My hope and strength are gone.
How long? How much longer?

Executioner, here's my neck: slaughter!
Take off my head like a dog's—you've got the ax
and the arm, and the world to me is a butcher's
    block.
We, whose numbers are small—
it's open season on our blood:
crack a skull, let the blood
of infant and elder spurt on your chest,
and let it remain there forever, and ever.

If there's justice—let it come now!
But if it should come after I've been
blotted out beneath the sky,
let its throne be cast down.
Let the heavens rot in evil everlasting,
and you, with your cruelty,
go in your iniquity
and live and be bathed in your blood.

And cursed be he who cries—Revenge!
Vengeance like this, for the blood of a child,

Satan has yet to devise.
Let blood flood the abyss!
Let it pierce the blackest depths
and devour the darkness
and eat away and reach
the rotting foundations of the earth.

Odessa, 1903

Early Work
(1890—1899)

Volozhin, Zhitomir, Korostyshev, Sosnowiec

> *"I'd stand at the yeshiva table for long hours, the sea roiling around me, the sea of Talmud, in which hundreds of mouths were shouting, enthusing, and intoning—and I would mouth the phrases, '[Rabbi] Abbaye said...' but my heart was elsewhere, in other worlds."*
>
> —BIALIK on Volozhin

To the Bird

Hello, little bird, back at my window
from lands where it's warm—
my soul has longed for the sound of your song
all winter while you've been gone.

Sing and tell me, my little bird,
of marvels in distant places;
if in the land of the sun as well
there's trouble, or something's gone wrong.

Do you bring greetings from brothers in Sion,
distant kin who are near?
Have they any idea, those joyful ones,
of just how deeply I suffer?

Do they know how wholly the tide
has turned against us here?
Sing, little bird, of wonders from where
spring springs eternal.

Do you bring greetings from the land and its fruit,
its valleys and ridges and plains?
Has God brought Sion compassion or comfort?
Is it still a place of graves?

And do the herb-filled hills and fields
of Sharon send up myrrh?
Has the oldest of sleeping woods woken?
Is Lebanon dozing or roused?

Does dew on the mountain fall like pearls?
If it falls are they also like tears?
And how are the clear Jordan's currents?
And all the mountains and hills?

Has the heavy cloud been lifted from them,
which spread a great shadow and gloom?
Sing, little bird, of the land where the living
fathers came to their end.

Are the flowers I planted flowering still,
while I myself am wilting?
I remember days like those when I blossomed—
though now I'm weakened and old.

Say, little bird, what secret words
those are that the bushes whisper.
Do they offer comfort, or hope ahead?
Does their fruit like Lebanon rustle?

Friends in labor, who sow with tears
and harvest sheaves in song,
lend me a wing to reach the land
where almonds and date palms bud.

And I, my bird, what could I tell you?
What would you hope to hear?
From *this* cold land song won't come,
only lament and despair.

Should I tell of trials already told
and known throughout the world?
Who could count the sorrows breaking
over us, wave after wave?

Fly little bird to your deserts and peaks,
be glad you've left my tent;
if you had stayed with me here you'd now
be weeping for my plight.

But weeping and tears are no cure
and will not heal my wound.
My eyes have dimmed, my tears been shed.
Like grass my heart has withered.

The tears have vanished and summers too;
but no end comes to my grieving.
You're back, little bird, hello, hello—
now lift your voice and sing.

Volozhin, 1890/91

My Return

Before me again, an old man,
the lines of his crumpled, wizened face—
a straw's shadow, bobbing like a leaf,
sinking and nodding over his pages.

Before me again, an old woman,
darning and knitting woolen socks,
her mouth busy with bitter curses
and her lips' twitching, which does not stop.

And, for years and years, our house cat
hasn't budged at all from his place—
deep in dreams beside the brazier,
he's come to terms, it seems, with the mice.

And in the darkness, as ever,
the warp and weft of cobwebs stretch,
thick with the swollen carcasses of flies
there in the corner, looking west.

For ages and ages nothing has changed—
from the brink of your time not a thing is new.
I'll come, my friends, and stay with you,
and together we'll rot till we stink.

1891 (1896)

A Summer Day

When the sun is high on a summer afternoon
and heats up the sky that becomes like an oven;
when the heart longs for a corner to dream in—
Come to me, weary one, come...

I've got a garden that's lush with sumac
and shady, and far from the crowds there's a knoll
enveloped in green that tells of God's secrets.
That's where we'll hide, my friend, and rest.

Delighting in that mystery's softness,
we'll savor the day's clues and its signs
as they're revealed, in a golden ray,
piercing layers of the shadows' gray.

And on a bleak wintery night,
as the black attacks you and the cold swirls,
and the frost's blades slice through your flesh—
Come to me...Lord...Come!

My house is small and has no trappings;
but it's bright, and open to a stranger.
In the hearth there's a fire; on the table, a candle.
Sit with me, friend—until you're warm.

Hearing the howling spirit of the storm,
we'll remember the poor in the street. They suffer.
Toward my heart, my friend, I'll press you
and shed a pearl of fealty, like dew.

But when autumn comes, with clouds and downpours,
and the world is desolate and the mud starts to ooze,
and the roof rattles, like a moth in the heart—
then leave me, friend, to myself.

Let me be—in that tedium.
My heart, consumed with decay, should see
no one, and no one would fathom, anyway,
the hollow silence of my grief.

Korostyshev, 1896

And the People Are Grass

For the spirit of the Lord bloweth upon it,
And the people are grass.

—Isaiah 40:7

And the people are grass, dry as a tree.
And the people are hollow, hollowed and heavy out to
    infinity,
where God's voice thunders from every quarter
and the people are not moved. And do not tremble.
And none rise like a lion, not a soul in pride is roused.
And no one shivers as the voice sounds within the heart of
    a city,
and none shudder in joy with those around them—
west and east, left and right, from sea to sea,
revealed in their being seeds of the living God
come from afar to the voice of the Lord.
And those who call in that Name, in faith and innocence,
are offered not a hand or word of concern.
In the roar of a people gone mad around their burnished
    idols,
the voice of God is drowned, his great thunder engulfed.
And spat at in disgrace, in the heart of the wicked
the Lord's word is mocked and scorned.

And the people are withered—full of venom and vanity,
rot and corruption from toe to skull.
No leader of heart with courage emerges
through this time of trial and distress,
heart aflame with a spark that would roil the blood
so a flare might shine from his eyes, showing the way
and bearing the name of the nation and its God
above the idols of gold and a silver emptiness—

holding within him a sliver of vision, abounding truth,
fierce power and hatred of life surrendered
to servitude and disdain, compassion vast as an ocean,
countless mercies lining the rift within his wretched nation
and heavy as its yoke. All this in his heart would pulse
and surge like the sea, all this in his blood like fire
burn and echo day and night, like thunder:
"Get up—to work. The hand of God is with us."

And the people have gone astray, seeking, it seems, disgrace
    and scorn,
their actions lacking foundation, their work knowing no law,
for thousands of years they've wandered, in exile greater
    than one could bear,
having left the heart to its wish, while from the nation
    counsel perished.
Inured to the rod that has beaten them, do they feel the pain
of the soul's affliction by foes, not just the lash of whip
    against skin?
Can they see beyond their moment's anxiousness
and through the dark valley of exile like an abyss?
Is the light envisioned? Can they bear the soul's burden for
    the day
to set its sights on the end, and show its generation a way?
Till the rod awakens them they will not be roused.
They will not rise till plunder comes.
A withered leaf from a tree, grass in a heap,
a parched vine, a rotting bud: Could dew revive them?
Even as the ram's horn blasts and the banner is borne,
can the dead be woken? What would stir the dead?

Sosnowiec, 1897

Midnight Prayer

A night of storms. Strong winds
roll a thick cover of clouds
over the small town, which sinks
deep into its sleep and mire.

The darkened alleys go silent, and still,
apart from the clattering rain pouring in,
as trembling and shaken homes, stunned,
here and there are being humbled.

And like a wretched orphan whom
the righteous forgot to offer shelter
and warmth, those without a roof
huddle and quietly groan

as though they're thinking or—dwelling
on dark thoughts they keep to themselves.
Have they dug their way to the foundations?
Called into question the entire design?

The rain pours down and down and splatters
like streams of tears against the wall;
the roofs grow gradually weaker,
and the whole town lets out a wail.

Through their dreams in the dark, sleepers
are cursing tomorrow, along with the past.
Easy now, leeches of the world—*schnorrers*!
Here's a dream: the people's task.

Between the gusts of wind there bursts
a howl that freezes the blood. *Ach!*
Who knows if it isn't the curse
of another good soul giving up.

Not a single star remains on high,
no bright spark or ray of valor;
a lone window glows there: a Jew
rising to his midnight penance and prayer.

Sosnowiec, 1898

Over Your Heart

The threshold edicts of your hearts are broken
and sullied, and so the demons prance—
and a chorus of clowns, disciples of folly,
within great storm clouds rave.

Can you see who's waiting there by the door
with a broom? The keeper of the ravaged shrines.
Despair—is coming, and the jubilant pack
will be expelled, swept out: "Move on."

The last glimmer of your fires will sputter,
your shrines go quiet, the crowds forgotten.
And over your hearts' barren altar,
desolation's cat will howl and yawn.

Sosnowiec, 1899/1901

The Middle Years, Part I
(1900–1903)

Odessa, Kishinev, Odessa

> *"Here can be found everything that an active, educated man might ever need."*
>
> —ODESSKII ALMANAKH, 1831

> *"Seven miles around Odessa burn the fires of hell."*
>
> —Yiddish popular saying

Zephyrs

Was it a mother's kiss—or sparrows'
chittering that broke off my honeyed dream?
I woke to sheaves of light that lashed
my cheeks and flashed into my eyes,
their lids thick with the webs of sleep,
cherubs clinging to the wall-trim still—
as the morning called, the day bustling,
and a cart clattered over the stones.

The nest on my windowsill stirred
then burst into a boundless clamor.
Warbling *Yes!* from the day's splendor,
the morning zephyrs were signaling to me,
prancing and sparkling, mischievously,
tapping like doves on the windowpanes,
sliding and slipping in the liquid light
that spread gently across my back.

Their faces radiant, they wink and hint:
Get up—hurry! Shine with us!
We'll laugh when simple joy ripples out.
And as for the light already splashed,
we'll toss it further, on and on—
to tassels of corn, and curling locks,
to stretches of water between the swells,
to an infant's smile in his mother's heart,
to drops of dew on a girl's cheek,
a child's tear, a butterfly's wing,
shards of glass and bubbles from soap,
a brass button, poetry's rhymes.

"Come out! Hurry! Get up! Shine!"
They wink and hint, their eyes lit,
their small faces' luster glowing,
their limbs swishing, airy and clear,
a warm light on my face shimmering.
And the heart melts! My eyes open,
then close—the light's rushing through me!

Come, zephyrs of innocence, come!
Under my radiant bright-white sheet!
We'll romp and rollick into the day;
across my soft skin you'll skip.
Come! onto my curls, my lips,
into my smile, the depths of my eye.
Wash through my heart and make me sheer.
Sink into my soul. And shine!—
And over me passes a sweet sort of slumber;
my veins and limbs fill with pleasure,
and the heart, flooded, overflows
and explodes like a fountain of brightness pouring—
sweetness! My eyelids open, and close—
Lord, the light's rushing through me!

Odessa, 1900

I Scattered My Sighs

I scattered my sighs to the wind,
    my tears soaked the sand:
if ever, wind, you find my brother,
    tell him I am a burnt-out brand.

Tell him a fountain of light flowed in me
    and little by little went dry.
In my heart a flame once glowed;
    then spark by spark it died.

Now my spring is like a wound—
    trickling at times and at times a flood;
and my heart in secret sends up smoke,
    banked in ash, and blood.

Odessa, 1901

Stars Glisten and Fade

Stars glisten and fade,
and in the dark, people decay;
look at it all, my friend,
in my heart—grays over gray.

And dreams bud and wither,
and hearts blossom and rot;
look at it all, my friend,
in my heart—rubble and loss.

And everyone's praying for light,
on lips that wilt with prayer;
and everything wearies in time
come back round again.

And the nights—how sluggish they are.
Even the moon now yawns—
drowsy, dented, and bruised,
worn out, waiting for dawn.

Odessa, 1901

Only a Line of Sunlight

Only a line of sunlight came through you—
suddenly, you were exalted, you'd grown—
your longing opened, and your flesh too:
  you'd ripened, like a heavy vine.

Only the storm of a single night
came through you, scattering your early crops;
and in your loveliness, godless dogs
  picked up, from afar, the scent of your corpse.

Odessa, 1901

The Sea of Silence Spits Out Secrets

The sea of silence spits out secrets
and all the world around it goes still;
and the roar of the river never ceases
behind the grinding stones of the mill.

Night's blackness closes in,
shadow begins to cover shadow.
Soundlessly, toward the sea of darkness,
star by star falls like an arrow.

And in the world's growing quiet,
I sense: my heart's awake and speaking.
I sense: a pure and single spring
welling slowly, reaching its brim.

Then my heart says to me, whispering—
"Your dreams are coming to pass, my son.
A star has fallen from the heavens,
but trust me—yours isn't that one.

Yours is still fixed on high
and in its way, as always, will rise.
It's flickering at you, sending comfort.
There it is . . . Lift your eyes."

And in the world's growing quiet,
I stare at my star, and think it a start.
All I have is a single world—
which is the world in my heart.

Odessa, 1901

Alone

The wind carried them into the light,
new song brightening their lives' mornings;
and I, a fledgling, was left, forgotten
beneath the Shekhinah's wings.

I was alone with that Presence,
her broken wing trembling over my head.
My heart knew hers—she feared for me,
her only child, her son.

Cut off from all corners, with only a small,
hidden, and desolate hollow remaining—
the House of Study—she took refuge,
and I was with her in sorrow.

My heart longed for the window and light,
as the space beneath her wing grew tighter;
her head fell to my shoulder, and her tear
slipped to my scripture's page.

She leaned against me in silence and wept
as though she were guarding me with her wing:
"The wind took them, they're all gone—
I've stayed on, alone..."

It was like the end of an ancient lament,
a prayer at once of entreaty and fear—
my ear hearing that quiet cry
and fathoming that scalding tear.

Odessa, 1902

I Didn't Win Light in a Windfall

I didn't win light in a windfall,
it wasn't bequeathed to me by my father;
I hewed it from a rock—I mined it
    from my heart's chamber.

A hidden spark in the stone of my heart,
one small spark, but—my own;
I didn't borrow or steal it from anyone.
    It's from me, and in me, alone.

And under the hammer of my great sorrow
that heart shattered, that rock of my mine;
and that spark flew—up to my eye,
    and from my eye to my lines.

And from my lines it flees to your hearts,
and in their flame it flares and moves on.
And I—I with the fat of my blood
    pay for what's consumed.

Odessa, 1902

News

The light clouds grow lighter,
the clear clouds still more clear—
avenues into a new
blue are being revealed.

I lift my eyes higher—
a curtain is being raised,
and with the heavens themselves
I'm speaking face to face.

Mouth to mouth, my heart's
channel opens to theirs:
and through the white luster
the sky's abundance pours.

Over my head that pure
azure is spilling into
the air, and through me like
Eden's balm and dew.

Already I can hear
the rustle of bright wings.
Already my heart feels
the rays along my veins.

Light, be fruitful and multiply,
startle my heart's walls—
and all at once, within me
new song starts to call.

Odessa, 1903

City of Slaughter

Get up and go to the city of slaughter and come to the yards
and see with your own eyes and run your hands along the
fences
and trees and stones, and across the walls' plaster, and
touch
the dried blood and stiffened tissue spilled from skulls of
the fallen.
And from there come to the ruins, step over the gouges,
pass by the pockmarked walls and bashed-in ovens
to the place where the hammer fell and fissures opened
baring the burnt brick and blackened stone which look
like gaping mouths, like dark and mortal wounds
that won't be dressed and will not know any balm.
Your feet will sink into feathers; you'll stumble over heaps
of slivers and shards, and the tattered remnants of books
and scrolls,
the fruit of great learning and labor and craft—obliterated, all.
But do not linger with that debris. Move on, along the road
where the acacia has come into bloom before you and the
air wafts
fragrance, the flowers like down, their scent like blood, and
your fury
notwithstanding, their strange incense ushers a softness
of spring into your heart—and it doesn't repulse you.
With ten thousand golden arrows, the sun pierces your liver
as, from each splinter of glass, seven rays glimmer with glee
in your doom—
for the Lord has called to the spring and the slaughter as one:
the sun rose, the acacia blossomed, and the slaughterer
slaughtered.

And you flee and come to a yard, where a mound swells—
across which lie a Jew and his dog—a single blade had
    taken their heads
and onto a single heap they were thrown, and through the
    mix
of their pooling blood pigs now rummage and wallow.
Tomorrow the rains will come and wash it into oblivion,
and the blood will cry no longer from the sewers and trash,
for into a great abyss it will drain, quenching a thornbush's
    thirst.
And all will be as nothing, as though it had never been.

Then up to the attics you'll climb, and stand in the dark,
the bitter fear of death lingering there in the silence and
    gloom;
as from dim holes, and the gables' shadows,
motionless eyes gaze at you... These are the spirits
of our "saints," wretched and desolate souls;
under a sloping roof they huddled, then spoke no more.
Here the hatchet found them, here where they'd gathered
    to seal
with final glances the great grief of their pointless deaths
and cursed lives. Trembling in terror, they embraced,
and from the place where they'd hid they issued their claim
on the world in silence, their eyes alone asking: Why?
Who but God on earth could bear this quiet?
And you lift your eyes to the roof's tiles. They are silent as
    well
and cast a pall across you as you turn to the spiders—
survivors, eyewitnesses, who tell you what they have seen:
bellies split and stuffed full of feathers,
nostrils and nails, hammers and skulls,
the slaughtered left to die under roofs—

an infant found sleeping by his butchered mother,
her breast gone cold, her nipple still in his mouth;
a sliced-open child whose soul let go with his final cry for
    his mother.
Here are his eyes too, calling my people to account.
These and more a spider reports—
skulls broken and brains showing through, enough to crush
your own spirit and soul, once and forever—
and you check yourself and choke back the howl
and bury it deep in your heart before it can out.
From there you leap up and leave—for the earth will do as
    it does—
and the sun, as of old, spills its light across the land.

Go down then into the murk of the cellars,
where the pure daughters of your people were ravaged
one by one—woman after woman, defiled under seven—
daughters in front of their mothers, mothers before their
    daughters' eyes,
before the slaughter, during the slaughter, after the
    slaughter.
Under your hand you feel the filthy blanket and the bloody
    pillow,
pits where wild boars had wallowed, stables for horse-like men,
their axes dripping with scalding blood.
And behold, in the dark of that same corner
beneath the mortar for making matzo, there behind the
    barrel,
husbands had huddled, grooms and brothers, peering from
    cracks
at the gasping sacred bodies beneath the flesh of mules—
choking in their impurity, gulping blood from their own
    throats.

As a man has at his meal, the abominable creatures had at
   their flesh:
they lay in their shame, and the husbands looked on and
   did not stir
and did not stab at their eyes or lose their minds,
though maybe they prayed in their way and their hearts:
"Lord of the world, bring on a miracle now, so this evil
   won't reach me."
And those who survived the defilement and woke from
   their blood,
their entire lives were debased as the light of their world
   was doused,
body and soul fouled forever, without as within—and their
   husbands
sprang from the hollows and ran to the house of their God
   and recited
in the name of their refuge and strength on high the
   blessing for miracles.
And the priestly line among them came forth, asking their
   sages:
"Rabbi, my wife? Is she ... 'permitted'? 'Forbidden'?"
And all was falling back into place, returning to what had
   long been.

And now I will show you where they were hiding:
latrines and styes, and other depressions of excrement;
see with your very own eyes where they lie,
your kin and your people's children, sons of the Maccabees'
   sons,
descendants of God Full of Mercy's lions, seeds of the
   saintly,
twenty souls to a single hole, and sometimes thirty times
   thirty.

And they made my glory great in the world and sanctified
    my name,
fleeing like mice in flight, concealing themselves like fleas,
they died the death of dogs, there where they were found,
the sole surviving son emerging, the morning after,
to find the bloody, trampled corpse of his father.
So why, son of man, are you weeping? And why bury
your face in your hands? Grit your teeth and be gone.

Go down again, follow the slope of the town and discover
by a garden a large enclosure: this is the killing's corral.
Like an enormous stare of owls, or camp of bats,
exhausted and drunk with blood, and draped across the
    slain,
wheels were scattered, wheels within wheels—
their spokes extending like fingers stretched out to murder,
their hubs soaked with blood and brains.
At the end of the day, as the sun in the west is setting—
veiled in clouds of blood and lined with a fire's flames—
open the gate and quietly enter that space
as darkness's terror drifts about you, an abyss of mysterious
    horror.
Fear. Fear all around—hovering there in the barn,
clinging to walls, preserved in the silence.
And beneath the mounds of wheels, from beyond the cracks
    and holes,
you sense skin twitching, crushed limbs in spasm,
souls contorted within their dying, lying in their blood—
the wheels heaped on their backs now moving.
And a last gasp goes out, a tortured sound failing,
as over their heads there hangs, as though congealed,
a dismal sorrow, sorrow everlasting, which holds, and
    trembles.

This is the spirit of brokenness itself, afflicted and greatly
    tried,
captive within its own prison and mired
in an ancient anguish, unwilling to leave it behind.
And a dark Presence, the Shekhinah, weary with grief and
    drained,
wafts into each corner but cannot find rest,
wanting to weep but unable, silent but longing to sigh—
and still in her mourning she would give in, and die in
    hiding,
her wings spread over the martyrs' shadows, one wing
    covering her head,
her tears concealed. Without a word, she weeps.

And you too, son of man, shut the gate behind you—
shut yourself into the gloom and look to the ground
and stand in your shame, becoming one with the sorrow
and letting it fill the life that you have left to live ...
And on that day when your soul is battered and its vigor
    abated,
that sorrow will be your refuge, and also a poison spring
in you like a curse, stirring like a ghoul.
Through you it will seep, and on you weigh like a nightmare.
In your chest you'll carry it—to the four corners of the sky,
and you'll try to find words to describe it. And fail.

Then wander on to the outskirts of town, to the place of
    rest-everlasting.
Not a soul will see you go; alone you'll pass
and stop at the graves of the martyrs and saints, old and
    young,
and stand there with their dust, as I cast a silence across
    you.

Your heart will rot from holding back your pain and disgrace,
and I'll hold back the tears in your eyes. And you'll know
the time to low has arrived, like an ox bound to the altar—
and I'll stiffen your heart and the groan won't come.
Here are the calves for the slaughter: here they lie, to a one.
And if there's a price for their lives, tell me what it might be.
Wretched of the earth, forgive me—your God's as impover-
    ished as you are:
impoverished in your living, and how much more so in your
    demise.
Tomorrow you'll seek your reward, knocking at my doors,
and I will open them: Look—I've nothing left to give.
I feel for you, my children, to you my heart goes out—
you offered yourselves for nothing, and you and I alike
know nothing of why you were killed or what for.
Your dying knew no reason, nor does your being alive.
And the Shekhinah? What does she say? She hides her head
    in a cloud
and, holding back the pain and disgrace, slips away, confused.
And I too by night, by night I go down to the graves
and stand there and stare at the slain, ashamed.
But as I live, said the Lord, I will not shed a tear.
Great is the pain, and great as well—the shame.
And which of the two is greater? Tell us that, son of man.
Or better yet—be still! Be my silent witness:
For in my disgrace you found me; you saw me in my
    distress.
And when you return to your people, do not go without a gift.
Bear them my abasement's rebuke, bring it down over their
    heads.
And with you take my wound—and plant it in their hearts.

And as you turn from the graves of the fallen,
the cushion of grass around them catches your eye.
It's soft, and moist as it is when spring begins, and you see
before you the buds of death and the graveyard's grass,
and you tear out a handful and toss it behind you, as if to
     say:
The people are grass. What hope is left for those torn away?
And you shut your eyes and see them no longer; but I will
     lead you back
from the graves of brothers who lived through the slaughter,
and with them you'll come on a day of fasting to the house
     of their prayer
and hear the cry of their brokenness, and be swept up by
     their tears
as the hall fills with wailing, with sobbing and mule-like
     moans,
and the hair on your flesh will be raised, as fear and
     trembling call you.
So the nation groans when its loss is great, and into its
     heart you gaze,
and lo—desert and waste. And if the anger takes shape
as vengeance, not a seed of it would survive,
not a single curse would come to fruition on those lips.
Are their prayers a fraud? Their wounds not real? Why the
     denial
on the day of their downfall? What good would deceiving
     me do?
But watch as they rot in their anguish,
as all descend into weeping and send up a great lament.
They pound their hearts and confess their transgression,
     saying:
We have strayed. And their hearts do not believe their
     mouths.

Could broken vessels transgress, or crushed pitchers of clay
    betray?
Why do they implore me then? Speak to them, so they'll cry,
thrusting a fist in my face as they make their case—
the insult of each generation, from the beginning and on—
and with their fists let them shatter the heavens and my
    throne.

And you, too, son of man, do not cut yourself off from the
    people—
believe the pain in their hearts, not the pleas on their lips.
As the prayer-leader lifts his voice: "Do this for those who
    were slaughtered,
for the infants and the toddlers..."—and with howls of
    sorrow
the hall columns shudder and the hair on your flesh
stands on end, and fear and trembling come through you.
I, I will be cruel: you will not wail with their tears.
And if your cry breaks forth, I'll crush it between your teeth.
They alone will profane their sorrow—you will not defile it
    for them.
For generations it will hold, a sorrow no lament could plumb;
your weeping will be checked, tears will not be spilled,
and around them you'll build a fortress, a steadfast iron wall
of murderous rage and hell's hatred and pent-up loathing.
In your heart it will root and grow, like a viper in its pit,
and from each other you'll drink that milk, and find no rest,
and starve the anger and make it thirst, and then destroy
    the wall,
and on the heads of cruel vipers it will be unleashed in time.
On a day of thunder, you'll send it against the people of
    your pity and wrath.

Now leave all that behind, and return at twilight to see
the end of the people's keening: Here are souls who woke
     trembling
at dawn, and returned by evening to the deepest sleep;
weary from weeping and broken in spirit they stand in the
     dark,
their lips still moving, muttering in prayer—their hearts
     parched,
no spark of hope inside them, no gleam of light in their eye.
A hand gropes in the gloom and seeks support—and there
     is none,
as after its fuel is spent, the burner's wick sends up smoke
and the old horse trundles on, its spirit long since broken.
If only a single word of condolence might release them
     from their grief
and bring them back toward life, and take them into the
     years that remain.
The fast is over. They've read *And Moses entreated*, and
     recited *Answer us*—
so why are the congregants dawdling? Will they read
     Lamentations as well?
No—a preacher has mounted the platform
and begun mumbling his bland pronouncements,
dressing the wounds in whispered verses.
Not a sound from on high could save them from him,
the smallest spark won't flare in their hearts.
And there the Lord's flock stands, old and young as one:
some listen and yawn, others nod in assent,
the mark of death on their foreheads, their hearts crushed,
their spirit dead, their vigor fled, their God gone.

But do not bemoan them and widen their wounds—
or increase their grief any further. They can bear no more.

Wherever your finger touches, there the wound is mortal.
Pain holds through their bones, and in their suffering
     they've grown old
and used to the shame. What good would condolences do
when pity on them is lost, and they are too wretched to
     rail at.
Let them be, move on. . . . Look—the stars have come out,
and the mourners, heads covered and cloaked in shame like
     thieves,
each with his heartbreak returns to his home—
back bent low, spirit emptier than ever—
each with his heartbreak climbs into bed,
corrosion along his bones, and rot deep in his heart.
And when, tomorrow, you rise and go on your way,
you'll see a horde of broken souls—groaning and sighing—
amassed at the windows of the wealthy, camped at their
     doors,
announcing their wounds to the world, like a peddler his
     wares:
one whose skull is cracked, another whose arm is gashed or
     bruised,
all extend a darkened hand, a shattered wrist—
their eyes the eyes of slaves, battered by masters,
and they say: "My skull is cracked, my father's a martyr—
     Please . . ."
And the wealthy, full of mercy, heap their mercies upon
     them,
reaching with sticks from their homes, dangling bundles
     above the skulls,
muttering *Good riddance* to themselves, as the beggars are
     consoled.
Off, beggars, to the graveyards—to dig up your forefathers'
     bones

and those of your martyred kin, to fill your sacks
and load them onto your shoulders, and set out on your
     way
and bring the bones as goods to the markets and fairs.
You'll find yourselves a place at the crossroads, for all to
     see,
and in the sun you'll spread your wares on rags filthy with
     excrement,
a beggar's song hoarse in your throat, as you sing of your
     stock, the dead,
and call for peoples' compassion, and pray for the nations'
     mercies.
And as you've sinned you'll sing, and grovel as you've
     groveled.
And now, son of man, why are you still here? Get up and
     flee
to the wilderness with your cup of grief and despair,
and rend your soul into pieces there
and feed your heart to an impotent fury;
and let your tears fall on the rocky lip of a cliff
and your bitter roar go out—and vanish, into the storm.

Kishinev and Gurovschina, 1903

The Middle Years, Part II (1903–1916)

Odessa, Warsaw, Odessa

> "Odessa encouraged. Warsaw rebelled."
>
> —FICHMAN

> "As for my impressions of Warsaw, I'll let you know in another letter. For now I can tell you that my heart is with Odessa."
>
> —BIALIK

From "Winter Songs"

A morning's chill and the crow's caw
woke me and—I rose early.
Suddenly, I have no idea why,
a kind of holiday joy slipped through me.

Who it was who sent that drop
into my heart I don't know,
or why all of a sudden I'm finding
my room so fine against the snow.

Rime has grown on the window!
That clear pane changed so fast—
last night it blossomed like Aaron's rod
or a small forest across the glass.

The drifts weigh on the stiff firs,
like pillars of palms or still-young oaks.
Hello, little plants of winter.
Huzzah for the crystal buds of frost.

A fresh, cold, and pure effulgence
filled my room and brought it to life—
as if, to honor a holiday, that night
an angel descended and painted it white.

That cold, fresh, serene splendor
soon filled my heart as well,
as though an angel of sheer extremities
had come through me to make it whole.

Odessa and Warsaw, 1903

The Word

Hurl the coals from your altar, prophet,
and leave them for the vile
to roast their meat and heat their cauldrons,
and let them warm their hands.
Cast the spark from your heart as well—
let it light cigarettes on their lips
and shine on sneers lying in ambush,
like thieves beneath their mustaches
and deep within their eyes' malice.
Here they come, the odious ones, and there they go,
the prayer you taught them on their tongue,
they feel your pain and hope your hope—
their souls long for the ruins of your altar
then swoop down and pick through the rubble
and salvage the broken stones
and sink them into the floors of their homes and garden walls
and set them up above their graves.
And if they find your charred heart in the wreckage,
they'll toss it to their dogs.

Kick over your altar out of shame—
let it collapse on its smoke and flames.
With a wave of your hand, sweep away the cobwebs
stretched across your heart like the strings of a harp
from which you'd woven a song of resurgence and salvation—
in fact a delusion and empty vision—
and cast them onto the wind to wander, torn and pure
in the space of the world, on a clear day at the end of summer.
One silver thread won't find another, or a web its like,
and with a day of driving rain, they'll vanish.

Your hammer of iron—cracked from pounding
hearts of stone in vain—
you'll beat into scraps for a shovel or hoe
with which to dig our grave.

And as for one who'd put God's rage on your tongue—
curse him without fear;
and even if your word is bitter, bitter as death,
or if it's death itself—we'll listen and learn.
Night's thickness surrounds us; look—the dark overwhelms,
and like the blind we grope.
Something has come to pass between us and no one knows
    what it is,
no one has seen or can say what has happened—
if the sun is rising or going down,
or if—for us—it has set forever.
And the chaos is great all around. And beyond the chaos,
    terror—
without refuge.
And if in the dark we vow or send up a prayer—
who would hear it?
And if in the name of God we curse,
over whose head will it hold?
And if we gnash our teeth, or lash out in anger with our
    fists—
on whose skull will that fall?
The void will swallow it all, the wind sweep it away;
and what is lost will be lost.
Nothing will help us now,
and there is no way out:
the heavens have gone dumb.
They know what they've done, and the grave will consume
    them.

In silence they bear their iniquity.
Prophet of the end, open your mouth,
and if you've something to say—
say it!
And if it's bitter as death, or even death itself—
say it!
Why be afraid of death? Its angel rides on our shoulder,
his bridle's bit between our lips—
as with blasts of joy, and cries of revival,
toward the pit we stagger.

Mrozy, near Warsaw, 1904

And If the Angel Asks

Where, my son, is your soul?—
"Wander in the world, my angel, and search for her!
There's a quiet village, somewhere,
encircled by a wall of woods,
its sky a pale blue and unbound
and at its heart its only daughter,
a solitary cloud, white and small.
One summer day, a child was playing,
a child left to himself and dreaming;
and I, my angel, was that child.
Once, the whole world buckled and grew still,
and the boy's eyes were drawn to the skies,
and they saw that pure brightness above,
and in that seeing his soul left him, leaving its cote like a
    dove,
for that gentle cloud."

—Did she fade away?—

"There's also a sun in the world, my angel!
My soul was saved by a ray of gold,
and on wings of splendor it glided for days
like a small white bird.
One morning she rode that merciful ray,
looking for a pearl of dew in the grasses;
a pure tear on my cheek trembled,
and the ray was shaken, and my soul fell
and sank with that tear."

—Did it dry up?—

"No, it fell on a page of sacred text—
my grandfather's warped and worn-out Talmud—
and in its fold were two white hairs from his beard,
threads from his tattered prayer shawl
and stains from dripping tallow and wax.
And in the Gemara, alone with those dead letters,
my soul was shaken."

—Was she smothered?—

"No, my angel, she fluttered and sang!
From these dead letters poems of life poured forth,
and on my grandfather's shelves, the dead stirred.
There were songs of all sorts—from a small, bright cloud,
a golden ray of light, a shining tear,
threadbare prayer shawls and melting wax.
But one song she didn't encounter—a song of early love.
She longed, seeking release, and found no consolation,
grew faint with yearning, constricted almost to death.
One day I opened the tattered book
and—my soul flew off.

"And still she flies and roams in the world,
wandering about but finding no rest.
And, on modest nights at the start of the month,
as the world blesses the sliver of moon,
she leans her wings against love's gate,
leans and knocks, weeping
secretly for love."

Warsaw, 1904

From "The Pool"

When I was young and my days were sweet
and the wings of the Presence first rustled over me,
my heart knew longing and mute amazement,
and I sought a secret place for its prayer.
And so, in the heat of the day, I'd sail
toward the kingdom of majestic calm
into the heart of the summer forest.
There among the trees of God
no echo of a falling ax was heard;
for long hours I'd wander a path
that only the wolf and hunter knew—
one with my heart and my god until,
stepping over the golden snares,
I'd enter the sacred shrine of the woods.

Beyond the veil of the leaves lay
a green island with a carpet of grass,
serene—a world unto itself,
a holy of holies among the shadows
of the forest's trunks and tangled canopies.
Its ceiling was a small blue dome
set down over the trees—
its floor was glass: a pool of water,
a silver mirror within the frame
of the damp grass, inside which lay
another and second, smaller world.
And in the middle of that dome
and at the center of that pool
facing stones of jacinth shone,
large and carnelian: two suns.

And as I sat at the edge of the pool
and gazed at the riddle of the twin worlds,
not knowing which was prior—
my head bowed beneath the blessing
of the ancient grove, the play of shadow
and light as one, of resin and song—
I'd feel, palpably, the silent flow
of a certain freshness enter my soul,
and my heart, thirsty for sacred mystery,
would slowly fill with quiet longing,
although it wanted more, and more,
and awaited the epiphany of His Presence.
Or that of Elijah. And I listened,
and my heart shuddered and nearly gave way,
as the echoed voice of a hidden God
exploded suddenly from the silence:
"Where art thou? . . ."
And huge wonder filled the forest,
and the oaks of God, firmly rooted,
looked on at me from within their majesty
in amazement: Who is this among us?

A silent language of gods exists,
a soundless speech of secrets, but rich
with color, the magic of shifting forms,
a fabulous spectacle. And within that language
God makes himself known to the chosen—
His spirit's elect. And the lord of the world
reflects as he will, and the artist gives shape
to the thoughts of his heart and dreams unspoken.
This is the language of vision, revealed
in an azure strip of the heavens' expanse
and within its silvery clouds and nimbuses

massed; in the corn's trembling gold
and the great cedar soaring—
the white wing of the fluttering dove,
and the broad strokes of the eagle's wings;
in the simple beauty of a man's back
and the splendor of the look in his eye;
in the sea's anger and its breakers' crash
and laugh; in the night's bounty and the silence
of falling stars; in the noise of fire
and the ocean-roar of daybreak's blaze
and dusk. Within this language, the language
of languages, the pool spelled out—for me
as well—its eternal riddle,
tranquil, and hidden there in the shade,
seeing all and also holding
and with it all always altering.
And so it seemed like an open eye
of the forest's lord—rapt in mysteries
and the deepest reverie.

Warsaw and Odessa, 1904–05

Bring Me in Under Your Wing

Bring me in under your wing,
   be sister for me, and mother,
the place of you, rest for my head,
   a nest for my unwanted prayers.

At the hour of mercy, at dusk,
   we'll talk of my secret pain:
They say, there's youth in the world—
   What happened to mine?

And another thing, a clue:
   my being was seared in a flame.
They say there's love all around—
   What do they mean?

The stars betrayed me—there
   was a dream, which also has passed.
Now in the world I have nothing,
   not a thing.

Bring me in under your wing,
   be sister for me, and mother,
the place of you, rest for my head,
   a nest for my unwanted prayers.

Odessa, 1905

From "Scroll of Fire"

1

Seas of flame roiled all night long, and tongues of fire leapt out over the Temple Mount. Stars scorched the sky, and sparks melted earthward. Had God kicked at His throne and shattered His crown?

Shreds of reddened clouds, laden with blood and fire, drifted across the wastes of night. Along the distant mountains, they told a tale of wrath, the wrath of a vengeful God, as His fury spoke from desert stones. Had He torn apart the crimson cowl of His throne and cast its rags to the wind?

Over those far-off ridges the fear of Him loomed, and a trembling took hold of the stones in their seething: The Lord is a God of Vengeance, the God of Vengeance has emerged!

And here that God of Vengeance is, in His glory, and His alone. Tranquil, awful, He sits on His throne at the core of the flaming sea. His cloak is a whirl of purple, burning embers are His footstool. Forks of fire crown Him, and a cruel frenzied dance surrounds Him. Above Him tongues of fire rage, gulping down the space of the world, while He sits, serene and frightful, arms folded over His heart. With a glance from His eye the blazes widen; the bonfires deepen as His eyelids twitch. *O blazing chargers, bring the dance to the Lord, bring to the Lord the dance of fury and fire.*

2

Dawn shimmered above the hills and gray vapors stretched through the valleys—the seas of flame grew calm, and the fiery tongues of His charred Palace were still.

Ministering angels gathered, as prescribed, in sacred choirs to sing the morning prayers. They opened heaven's windows and sent their leader to the Mount to see—had the doors to the Temple been opened and the cloud of incense wafted out?

And they saw the Lord of hosts, the Ancient of Days, sitting in the dawn's glimmer, gazing into the devastation. His cloak was a pillar of smoke, and His footstool dust and ashes. Between his arms His head was bowed, and rolling hills of grief overwhelmed Him. He sat, silent and desolate, looking onto the ruins. An anger of the ages darkened His brow, and a great stillness froze in His eyes.

Smoke hung over the Mount. Heaps of ash whispered and swelled, knolls of cinders and smoking embers, mound after mound, their sparks like banks of crystal and rubies there in the dawn.

And the lion who'd crouched and lain night and day by the altar, he too had gone quiet and vanished. Only a single orphaned wisp of smoke at the edge of the rubble curled, dying over the blackened stones into the morning silence.

And the ministering angels knew what God had done. They were shaken, and with them the morning stars shuddered. The angels covered their faces with their wings, afraid to look directly into God's sorrow.

That morning their song gave way—to a silent lament, a still small cry. They dispersed and wept, angel by angel, each one alone, as the world in silence wept with them....

And a single sigh, soft and deep, rose from the end of the world and spread—it was broken only by the weeping.... The heart of the world too had broken, utterly, and God could hold Himself back no more. He woke, roared like a lion, brought His hands together in a thunderous clap, and the Glory rose up over the ruins, and withdrew, into secret places...

Odessa, 1905

Summer Dies

Summer dies into choice
gold and amber, and the purple
of autumn gardens and twilight clouds
wallow in their blood.

The park empties. Only a few
stragglers linger—their eyes
lifted in longing toward the last
pass of the storks' caravans.

The heart's an orphan. Soon, in the stillness,
rain will tap at the window:
"Have you checked your shoes? Patched your jacket?
Go, get the potatoes ready."

1905

I Knew on a Night of Thick Darkness

I knew on a night of thick darkness I'd suddenly fade like a
    star
and not a star would know where I lay
although my rage would smolder, like a volcano
long after its flame had died,
and live among you, till thunder forever abandons the sky
and anger releases the ocean's waves.
If only your great grief could be gathered
and stored in the heart of the world—
it would fill the furrows of heaven and the fields,
pulse through the grasses and stars on high,
live in them, and with them evolve and be made new,
and like them wither and then revive, and flower
with neither homeland, name, or form—
a witness to your affliction down through the last
    generation,
without so much as a sound, or word, it would call to hell
    and the heavens
and keep redemption of the world at bay;
and when, at the end of days, the sun of self-righteous
    duplicity
rises over the graves of the fallen,
and hypocrisy's banner, dyed with your blood and arrogant
    under the skies, flutters over your slaughterers,
and the Lord's false seal engraved on that banner
drills through the eyes of the sun,
and the dance of pride and the trumpet-blast of deceit's feast
rattle your sacred bones in their graves—
and heavens' splendor shudders and with your grief goes
    suddenly dark,

as your innocent blood stains the sun,
a mark of Cain on the brow of the world, a sign of the
　　failure
of God's broken arm—
then star to star will tremble: Here it is—the Great
　　Delusion!
And here is your Great Grief!
And the God of Vengeance, his heart wounded, will rise up
　　and roar—
and set out with his terrible sword.

Odessa, 1905/1906

Dusk

Again the sun rose and again it set—
and again I did not see it,
and again a day, or two days—not even
a sign along the horizon.

At the edge of the west, a kind of vagueness,
and again the clouds have amassed:
Are worlds, O wise ones, being built there
    now—
or are they being erased?

Nothing is being built there, or razed;
my eye is taking it in:
the evening of idiot confusion has come,
dispersing its ash through the world.

And know, too, I sought your brass
and lost sight of my gold,
as the Demon King behind me grinned
his cruel smile of old.

1907

And When Days Grow Long

from the Visions of the Latter Prophets

And when days grow long—one slipping into the next as
    of old,
today like the day before yesterday and on,
ordinary days of scant satisfaction and great weariness—
and a man at twilight goes out to the shore to gather his
    thoughts
and sees that the sea doesn't flee—
he yawns;
and then he considers the river, the Jordan hasn't changed
    its course—
and he yawns;
and he notes that the Pleiades and Orion haven't budged
    from their places—
and he yawns;
and together they lie, man and beast in their boredom—
the burden of their lives heavy upon them,
the man picking at hairs in his tedium,
and the cat's whiskers wearing thin.

And the longing burgeons,
wafting up like must from mold,
rising from rotting wood;
it fills every crack and hole in a home,
like lice spreading through rags.
And a man goes home for his evening bread
and dips its crust into vinegar, with his salted fish—
and longs;
and he drinks from his murky lukewarm cup—
and longs;

and he takes off his shoe and sock at the edge of the bed—
and longs.
And they sit and long as one, the man and his beast,
the man in his dream, within the folds of his longing
     whimpering,
as the cat claws at his roof and wails.
Then the hunger comes,
swelling and gnawing like no other,
hunger for neither bread nor vision, but—for the Messiah!

And morning after morning just before sunrise,
a man in his bed and beneath his ceiling stirs—
crushed with wandering, sated with dreams and empty on
     waking,
with troubled sleep still caked on his eyelids
and night's terror in his bones,
as the cat scratches and yowls,
picking at its belly and skull—
and he rushes to the window to wipe off the vapor
or stands at his threshold, shielding his eyes with his
     hand,
then lifts a bleary, bloodshot eye, craving salvation,
toward the path behind the yard
and the hill of trash in front of his house—
and he seeks— the Messiah!
And his wife wakes with the blankets strewn,
her hair disheveled, her body aching and her spirit dark,
and she wrests her shriveled teat from an infant's lips
and tilts her head to listen intently:
Isn't that...the Messiah coming?
Wasn't that his donkey braying?
And a toddler raises his head from a crib
and a mouse peers from its hole:

Is *that* the Messiah coming?
Wasn't that jangling his donkey's harness?
And the servant girl blowing on the coals by the stove
sticks her blackened face out the window:
Is the Messiah coming?
Wasn't that the blast of his horn?

1908

Before the Bookshelf

Old tomes, and sleepers lying in dust,
accept these greetings, these kisses from my lips.
My soul's returned from sailing to distant islands,
and like a wandering dove, weakened and trembling,
she flutters down to the nest that she once knew.
Do you recognize me? It's only me—anyone—
child of your fold ever since, and Nazirite to life.
Of all the precious things God set on earth,
my early days and youth knew you alone.
In the heat of a summer noon, you were a garden—
and from my beginnings a comfort on winter nights,
as thick pages I studied shielded my spirit
and I learned to slip my dreams between your lines.
Do you remember? Still? I haven't forgotten.
At the desolate house of study, in an upper room,
I was the last of the last ones, and on my lips
my fathers' prayers flickered and passed away,
as there, in a hidden corner beside your shelves,
before my eyes the lamp of eternity dimmed.
In those days, when I was still just a boy
and soft down had yet to graze my cheeks,
winter nights would find me, in the small hours,
over an ancient book and its splitting skin,
alone with my soul's dreams and with its fears.
Its amber glimmer before me still on the table,
the lamp with its kerosene stood, its wick blackened.
A mouse picked its way on one of the shelves,
and the hearth's ember whispered its final hiss.
And I—my flesh shivered with the fear of God;
my teeth clattered with the terror of death.

It was a night of dread, a night accursed.
Outside, beyond the blind eye of the window,
an angry storm was howling and whirling, and wailing;
shutters snapped—iron latches and all—
and demons shook the walls from the pit below.
My fastness was being shattered before me, and I saw
as well the Lord's Glory fleeing from where
she'd hidden behind the curtain of the Ark,
and my grandfather's figure—a shadow and shelter beside me,
witness and silent judge to my heart's desire—
that too was slipping from view and escaping,
and only the flame of my candle, fading, remained.
Back and forth it fluttered, then leapt to its end.
All went suddenly black, and the window burst open,
and I, a tender fledgling, was thrown from his nest
into the realm of night and its darkest places—

Now, ages and ages, it seems, have passed.
My brow is furrowed, and so too is my soul,
and the wheel of my life has turned and taken me back
and set me before you again, secrets of the shelves,
heirs of Lvov, Slavita, Amsterdam, Frankfurt;
my hand turns your heavy pages once more,
and my tired eyes search between your lines,
looking in silence among the letters' crowns,
trying to catch there a trace of my soul and find
a path—toward the place of her first flitting,
where she was born and knew that she was home.
See, my guides, how my heart goes quiet:
not a tear trembles on my eyelid now.
I look around and don't know who you are;
and you—no longer stare from your letters
into my soul's abyss with open eyes,

the doleful eyes of the ancient elders,
and I can fathom your lips' whispers no more,
which speak from a grown-over grave, long forgotten.
Your rows are a necklace of black pearls to me now,
their cord broken. All your pages are widowed,
each and every letter left an orphan.
Have my eyes weakened? Has my hearing failed?
Or have you rotted away, dead to the world,
and nothing of you remains in the land of the living
while I, in vain, like a thief tunneling
without a candle or lamp, have groped with a spade
into holes in the ground and the darkest places,
digging night and day in search of your graves,
anxiously seeking—around their roots and beyond them—
hidden signs of life, and life in signs,
while they in fact are far above and alive
in every city and people, pulsing on slopes
and before the eyes of all and the rustling trees.
Seven times they returned to their dance,
their roar crossing the borders of every sea
as . . . not even an echo reached my ears.

And, who knows,
if not for my going out to the night's domain,
to caves of the people's graves and the spirit's ruins,
nothing would have been saved or gained at all,
apart from this spade, still in my tired hands,
and this ancient dust beneath the nails of my fingers.
If I'm no weaker or emptier than I was,
I'll spread my hands before the glory of the night
and look for a path to its heart's mysteries,
a soft refuge in the black wings of its cloak,
and call to it, weary almost to death: "Come,

gentle glory of the night, gather me in.
Don't deny me—me, a refugee of graves.
I want rest, for my soul—the quiet of eternity."

And you, stars of God, faithful interpreters
of my heart, why are you silent? Why now?
Does your gold's eyelid hold not even a word
or faint clue for the heart within me? Or maybe
it does—and I no longer remember its language,
no longer understand what you are saying
through those letters and with your secrets and hints.
Answer me, stars of my strength, my God, my sadness.

near Odessa, 1910

A Small Branch Sank

A small branch sank and came to rest
on a fence—so I've been sleeping:
the fruit has fallen—what's it to me,
or to the trunk of my tree?

The fruit has fallen, the flower's forgotten—
though the leaves live on;
a storm is stirring, and soon they'll lie
lifeless along the ground.

And then—drawn-out nights of terror:
no rest for me, no sleep.
Against the wall of the dark I'll pound
my head, and struggle.

Spring will bloom; I'll be alone,
dangling from my tree—
a bare branch without bud,
and neither fruit nor leaf.

Odessa, 1911

He Gazed and Died

He entered the orchard's mysteries, a torch in hand,
     and fifty gates to pass through,
and trials at every turn—abyss within
     abyss, and mountains on mountains.

At every gate swords flashed, and beyond
     the doorposts serpents were lurking.
He crossed in peace, stepping over the snakes
     and bending beneath the blades

as he sped on, his torch held high before him,
     and angels, amassed and amazed,
withdrew in silence: Would he make it alive
     through to the final gate?

He would try. And he reached the mystery of mysteries,
     to which no stranger had come,
and aimed for the edge of endlessness where, at root,
     antitheses were one.

Ahead he forged, and found the straightest of paths,
     which doubled back and around;
he took it and...arrived in time to a place
     with neither place nor time

and reached the end of darkness and light: the void,
     where no eye held sway,
and the fiftieth gate, the last one—God in hiding—
     was still very far away.

The torch sputtered as the path coiled—the approach
        grew harder and harder.
All was a corridor to corridors: What of the final
        gate and the sacred chamber?

His soul flagged. His eyes no longer reliable,
        his spirit began to falter;
he could make it upright no further,
        and on his belly he crawled,

dust on his tongue, a last plea on his lips
        burning to the end:
"If only I could get to the fiftieth gate
        and see beyond the curtain..."

The prayer was heard. And before the torch died out,
        he arrived at the cusp—
the fiftieth gate, a threshold of the purest marble,
        appeared at the edge of the void.

He trembled, his eye struck by the splendor: Should he knock?
        He waited. And a moment longer.
In him suddenly the courage surged, and he rose,
        and then—he did knock...

And the torch went out. The gate's doors opened
        and he glanced within—as his body,
sinking beside a smoking ember, stretched
        over the X of the deep.

Odessa, 1915–16

Poems for Children
(1922–1934)

Berlin, Tel Aviv

> "The creation of a natural literature for the young in
> a language that isn't truly their mother tongue
> depends more than anything on 'fortune,' almost on
> a kind of 'mercy from on high.'"
>
> —BIALIK

At the Gate

A dove is longing
a dove that's fair,
on boat-wings that dove
will lead me there
across the sea
to the land I love.

Tell me, O waves,
where the fish are teeming,
how could I reach
that land while I'm dreaming
and the door is locked
and my key is broken?

Not a word was heard.
So a boy with his bird
knocking waits—
still at those gates.

Berlin, 1922/23

That Bird Has a Nest

That bird has a nest
up in a tree,
and in it are eggs:
One...two...three!

And in each egg—
Shshsh!!! You'll wake them—
the *tiniest* chick
lies sleeping...

Berlin, 1922/23

The Potted Flower

From the sill
the potted flower
all day long
looks out over

toward his friends
in the garden beds
while here he stands
alone instead

Berlin, 1922/23

Song of the Birds in the Woods

Out to the woods once I went
and there I found a whirl of birds,
a whirl of birds great and small,
all pouring forth their song.
One began, calling: *eeee!*
All responded—*eeee, eeee, eeee!*
My maker's praises speak through me...

Out to the woods once I went
and there I found a whirl of birds,
a whirl of birds great and small,
all pouring forth their song.
Another started, crying: *awwww!*
All responded: *awww, awww, awww!*
Are you asleep, arise and call...

Out to the woods once I went
and there I found a whirl of birds,
a whirl of birds great and small,
all pouring forth their song.
A third began, saying: *leee!*
All responded: *leee, leee, leee!*
The Lord is here to help me, truly...

Out to the woods once I went
and there I found a whirl of birds,
a whirl of birds great and small,
all pouring forth their song.
Another started, calling: *teee!*
All responded: *teee, teee, teee!*
Lo, He is my surety...

Berlin, 1922/23

Flower to Butterfly

Butterfly, butterfly—
your flower flies!
Land on me lightly,
between my two eyes.

Land on me gently,
I'll show you the view
from the edge of my cup,
as you sip your dew.

Sew from my petals
a coat to deploy,
with fabulous patterns
and wings of sheer joy.

Are we both flowers?
Siblings? Of course!
Your flower's mine,
and my flower's yours!

before 1925

Across the Sea

Across the sea
across the sea,
do you know, little bird,
which way that might be?

Across the sea
in a land by the sea
where the islands are golden—
their names now escape me—

in isles of gold,
across the sea,
giants are roaming,
a people that's worthy;

a people that's simple,
upright, and strong;
and they have a king
who never does wrong.

The king has gardens
across the sea,
birds of Eden
nest there in peace.

Across the sea
across the sea,
do you know, little bird,
which way that might be?

before 1924

See-Saw

See, saw, see, saw,
down and up, up and down!
What is up?
What is down?
Only I,
you and I—
both of us balanced
on the scales
there between
the earth and sky.

Odessa, Berlin, Tel Aviv(?), 1906/1933

ACKNOWLEDGMENTS

Serious thanks to the friends and colleagues who helped this book into being during an especially challenging time: first, last, and always—Adina Hoffman; and generously in between: Shahar Bram, Joshua Cohen, Robyn Creswell, Edwin Frank, Eli Gottlieb, Zali Gurevitch, Arik Kilemnik, Konstanze Kunst, Gabriel Levin, Feisal Mohammed, Meghan O'Rourke, Haviva Pedaya, Robert Schine, the late David Shapiro, Richard Sieburth, Eliot Weinberger, Rosanna Warren, Christian Wiman, Graeme Wood, and Steven Zipperstein.

NOTES

Hebrew versions of all the poems in this volume can be found in *H. N. Bialik: Poems* (with introductions, notes, and supplements), edited by Avner Holtzman (2004). I've also consulted Dan Miron's three-volume critical edition of Bialik's poems (1983, 1990, 2000). Digital versions of almost all of Bialik's poetry and prose, and some of his correspondence, are available on the Ben Yehuda Project website at https://benyehuda.org/author/89. Throughout my work on this book, I've turned to many more sources than I can list here, but the following Hebrew works have been especially central: *The Letters of Hayim Nahman Bialik* (1937–1938); *Complete Works of H. N. Bialik: Poems, Short Stories, and Essays* (1961); *Talks and Lectures*, vols. I and II (1935); *Uncollected Works* (1971); and *Poems and Songs for Children*, with illustrations by Nahum Gutman (1933). See also, in English, *Revealment and Concealment: Five Essays*, afterword by Zali Gurevitch (2000).

Useful biographies and biographical studies in English include David Aberbach's *Bialik* (1988); Sara Feinstein's *Sunshine, Blossoms, and Blood: H. N. Bialik in His Time* (2005); and Avner Holtzman's *Hayim Nahman Bialik: Poet of Hebrew* (2017).

Helpful critical work in Hebrew includes Yaakov Fichman's prose, especially *Writers in Their Lives* (1942) and *On Bialik's Poetry* (1946); A. Avital's *Bialik's Poetry and the Bible* (1952); Haim Orlan's *The Poetry of H. N. Bialik: An Anthology of Commentaries, Essays, and Studies on the Poet* (1971); *Bialik: Critical Essays on His Works*, edited by Gershon Shaked (1974); Ziva Shamir's *Not for Adults Only: Children's Literature by H. N. Bialik* (1986); Dan

Miron's *When Loners Come Together: A Portrait of Hebrew Litera-ture at the Turn of the Twentieth Century* (1987); *In the City of Slaughter, a Visit at Twilight: Bialik's Poem a Century After*, by Dan Miron, Mikha'el Gluzman, and Hannan Hever (2005); Zali Gurevitch's *Let man de-falig: Hayim Nahman Bialik* (2018); and Hamutal Bar Yosef's studies of Bialik's work in *The Russian Con-text of Hebrew Literature* (2020). See, too, the complete versions of the interviews for the documentary *Bialik: King of the Jews* (2014), directed by Yair Qedar, on "The Hebrews" project website: https://ivrim.co.il/en/

The following critical works in English have also been instructive at key junctures: *The Modern Hebrew Poem Itself*, edited by Stan-ley Burnshaw (1989); Alan Mintz's *Khurban: Responses to Catas-trophe in Hebrew Literature* (1996); all of Dan Miron's writing on Bialik, including Miron's introduction to *Songs of Bialik*, trans-lated by Atar Hadari (2000) and *H. N. Bialik and the Prophetic Mode in Modern Hebrew Poetry* (2000); Monty Noam Penkower's articles "The Kishinev Pogrom of 1903: A Turning Point in Jewish History" (2004) and "The Silences of Bialik: Israel's Bard Confronts Eretz Israel" (2006); Steven J. Zipperstein's *Pogrom: Kishinev and the Tilt of History* (2018), as well as his *Jews of Odessa: A Cultural History, 1794–1881* (1985) and *Elusive Prophet: Ahad Ha'Am and the Origins of Zionism* (1993); Hillel Halkin's *Lady of Hebrew* (2020); Hamutal Bar Yosef's English-language journal articles treat-ing the Russian context of Bialik's work; and Michael Stanislawki's "Jabotinsky's Early Zionism from 'In the City of Slaughter' to *Alien Land*," in *Zionism and the Fin de Siecle: Cosmopolitanism and Nationalism from Nordau to Jabotinsky* (2001). Other full-length collections of Bialik's work in English translation have been as-sembled by L. V. Snowman (1924), Israel Efros (1948), Ruth Nevo (1981), Steven L. Jacobs (1987), Atar Hadari (2000), and David Aber-bach (2004).

Bialik's poems are saturated with biblical and rabbinic allusions; these notes cite them only when they're most directly relevant to the English. On the whole, my comments focus on contextual information that might open the reading of the poems onto their contemporary cultural matrix, and in some cases onto our own. Unless otherwise indicated, dates at the end of each poem are for the year of composition.

Introduction

Information in the introduction is drawn from the following sources:

EPIGRAPH

Edward Said, *Freud and the Non-European* (2003), pp. 26–27.

PART I

Kishinev: Zipperstein (2018), especially p. 61ff. for an account of the Kishinev pogrom; and Zipperstein (1993), p. 201: "The word Kishinev...emerged as a metaphor for the vulnerability of European Jewry and for the inadequacy of standard Jewish response to oppression." See also Penkower (2004).

Even the most reluctant: The speaker is Pesakh Auerbach, who served as Bialik's assistant. Feinstein (2005), p. 102.

The day on which this great poem: Fichman (1946), p. 60. A literal translation of the title would be: "In the City of Slaughter [Killing]."

astonishing, austere, and pathbreaking: Mintz (1996), pp. 129–54, especially: "It can be argued, moreover, that within the entire canon of modern Hebrew and Yiddish literature, 'In the City of Slaughter' is the text that had the greatest direct impact on the formation of political attitudes and actions—for good or for ill." See also Mintz, "Kishinev and the Twentieth Century," *Prooftexts* 25, no. 1/2, pp. 1–8.

founded on a lie... to rouse: In other words, Bialik's call was to an awakening and strengthening, but not one that would turn Jews into mirror images of their oppressors. On the extension of both "City of Slaughter" and "On the Slaughter" into the charged post–October 7 context, cf. Nietzsche: "Whoever fights with monsters should see to it that he does not become one himself," *Beyond Good and Evil*, translated by Judith Norman (2002), p. 69.

Mendele Mocher Seforim: Steven J. Zipperstein, *The Forward*, July 7, 2014.

Kafka: Kafka's *Diaries*, trans. Ross Benjamin (2022), p. 45; Benjamin Ivry, *The Forward*, January 23, 2023; and Dan Miron, *Haaretz*, November 24, 2008.

lost Jewish communities: Oleg Budnitski and Timothy J. Portice, *Russian Jews Between the Reds and the Whites: 1917–1920* (2012), p. 217.

Netanyahu: *Haaretz*, June 30, 2014; Netanyahu's Twitter feeds and posts for June 30, 2014, and October 7, 2023; and Leon Wieseltier, *Liberties Journal* (Winter 2024).

not a pogrom: Zipperstein to me in a private communication in May 2024, and in an essay being prepared for publication.

Gaza: on Palestinian deaths, see Stephanie Nolen, *New York Times*, January 14, 2025; and on the numbers of displaced persons, see Human Rights Watch Report, "Hopeless, Starving, Besieged," November 14, 2024, as well as more recent accounts.

Rashid Hussein: Hussein eventually left Israel/Palestine and died in 1976, impoverished, in a fire in his New York midtown apartment. He was forty-one. His translations from Bialik were commissioned by a series sponsored by the Hebrew University and published by Dvir (the press Bialik founded with Ravnitzky). He was proud of the assignment, writes Adina Hoffman, and he himself observed that "whoever denies us [Arabs] the right to express our suffering and our hopes must also deny Bialik and [Sha'ul] Tchernikovsky [another important Hebrew-language Russian-Jewish poet] most of their nationalistic poems." See Hoffman, *My Happiness Bears No Relation to Happiness: A Poet's Life in the Palestinian Century* (2009), p. 266. Also Elliott Colla's blog post for May 14, 2021, which includes several of Colla's translations of Hussein's work, including this passage: "Without a passport / I've come to you / I've revolted against you / Stand up, and slaughter me! / So that I might feel what it is like to die without a passport."

by no means a poetry of appeasement: Fichman (1946), p. 213, and Orlan (1971), p. 248.

neutrality: Kenneth Moss writes about the "anti-party principle of Jewish cultural circles at the time." Bialik himself was very much a unifying force, though he remained a disciple of Ahad Ha'Am and, when it came to hard-core politics, leaned toward Chaim Weizmann's moderate faction. Over time he became increasingly harsh in his denunciations of Revisionist ideology. Moss describes Bialik's "political camp" as aligned with the "mainstream, nonsocialist" Zionism of the day. Moss, *Jewish Renaissance in the Revolution* (2009), p. 83ff. See also notes to the two Kishinev poems that follow below.

Rübner: in Burnshaw (1989), pp. 33–34.

worse than Satan: Ariel Hirschfeld in *Haaretz* (Hebrew), November 7, 2014; also Penkower (2006), pp. 252–63.

PART 2

a broad face: Fichman, *Shirat Bialik* (1946), p. 1; translation based on Feinstein (2005), p. 9.

melodic: Fichman (1942), p. 56.

risky efforts in Moscow: Bialik eventually secured permission to leave the country after a 2 a.m. meeting with foreign minister Georgii Chicherin. As Hamutal Bar Yosef tells it: "[At one point, Chicherin asked him] why such learned and idealistic people as themselves were not interested in helping to construct the 'magnificent edifice that is being built here for the benefit of humanity.' Bialik replied forcefully: 'Excuse me, sir, but we Jews have a different view. According to our belief, it is not possible that out of bad will grow good. How can we believe in hope for humanity when we daily see the blood of innocents being shed and human dignity so cruelly trampled upon" (Bar Yosef, "Bialik and the Russian Revolution," *Jews in Eastern Europe* [Spring 1996], pp. 19–20). Here too the ironies abound as we read Bialik's poems today.

PART 3

Yiddish speaks itself and *Scholem*: Harshav, *Language in a Time of Revolution* (1993), p. 86.

The energy, the moral sincerity: Aberbach (1988), p. 50.

my soul is rooted in the diaspora: Bialik, *Letters*, vol. I (1937), pp. 180–81, and in Holtzman (2017), p. 97.

Jewish dualism: Bialik, *Revealment and Concealment* (2000). Also Moss (2009), pp. 173ff.

coupling: Yeshurun Keshet in Orlan (1971), pp. 346–47.

aggadah *a smile*: Bialik, *Revealment and Concealment* (2000), p. 45.

A people whose fate is determined: Bialik, *Revealment and Concealment* (2000), p. 38.

Saramago: "To Write Is to Translate," in *The Translator's Dialogue: Giovanni Pontiero*, edited by Pilar Orero and Juan Sager (1997).

Jabotinsky's selection: Published in 1911. See Danielle Drori, "A Translator Against Translation: David Frishman and the Centrality of Translation in Century Hebrew Literature and Jewish National Politics," in *Transformative Translations in Jewish History and Culture*, edited by Markus Krah et al. (2019). To add to the compounded ironies, Jabotinsky is often credited with having come up with the phrase "From the river to the sea." The Revisionist program in fact called for that and more—i.e., settlement on *both* sides of the Jordan River. See Stanislawski (2001), pp. 190ff.

widespread recognition: Bialik's representation of the Jewish predicament seems to have rippled out even to Marina Tsvetayeva and into her famous, spiked, and increasingly unnerving formulation that "all poets are Jews," as she wrote in a section of her

"Poem of the End" (1923), which invokes pogroms—prominent among them, presumably, Kishinev.

Gorky: See his 1916 review in Hebrew translation by M. Basok at https://benyehuda.org/read/16642.

PART 4

a desolate plain of dry bones: Bialik, "The Sephardic Renaissance" (1961), pp. 235–36

From all the branches of our literature: Bialik, "The Hebrew Book" (1961), p. 212

Dryden: *Sylvae*, preface.

as I've made these translations: Apart from a few of the "poems of wrath," most of Bialik's work employs full rhyme and a wide range of accentual meters that suited the Ashkenazic pronunciation of his Hebrew. While I've listened throughout for the cadence and flow of his poems—to their textures, tensions, and viscosities—I've sought to sound salient aspects of their acoustic fields rather than attempting anything like a one-to-one mapping of their music. For more on Bialik's employment of meter, see Benzion Shalom's "Bialik's Meters," in *Bialik: Critical Essays*, edited by Gershon Shaked (1974); see also Harshav, *Three Thousand Years of Hebrew Versification* (2014).

providential addressee: Osip Mandelstam, "On the Addressee" (1913), in *Osip Mandelstam, Complete Critical Prose*, edited by Jane Harris et al. (1997), p. 45.

undervoicings . . . of loss: Hardy, "A Commonplace Day."

Poems

ON THE SLAUGHTER (על השחיטה)

This poem was Bialik's immediate response to news of the 1903 pogrom in Kishinev. See introduction and notes there. Publication of the poem in the leading Hebrew literary journal of the day, *HaShilo'ah*, was delayed by the Russian censor, despite the editor having added twenty-five rubles to the envelope into which he tucked the poem as he sent it to St. Petersburg for clearance. Both the title and the line "it's open season on our blood" had to be altered: the offending phrase was adjusted, and the new title simply repeated the opening line of the poem. Bialik's original title, which was eventually restored on book publication, embeds a brutally ironic allusion to the Hebrew blessing said before ritual slaughtering to sanctify the act and make the meat kosher: "Blessed art thou, O Lord, King of the Universe, who has sanctified us with his commandments and commands us on the slaughter[ing]." During the Middle Ages, the prayer was sometimes recited by Jews who preferred to take their own lives rather than be slaughtered by Christians (see Stanislawski, 2001, p. 185). Key biblical allusions bind line 8 to Psalms 94:3: "Lord, how long shall the wicked, how long shall the wicked prosper"; and line 24 to Ezekiel 16:6: "And when I passed by you, and saw you wallowing in your own blood, *I said unto you when you were in your blood, Live.*" That image of wallowing or bathing or being cleansed in blood is followed by the most famous and notorious lines of the poem. Their politicized misreadings notwithstanding, the sense seems clear, if nuanced: vengeance is not something to be determined by human agency. See also *Sanhedrin* 6b: "Let the law pierce the mountain"—indicating the supremacy of the law, or teaching, whereas in Kishinev it is blood that penetrates to the rotting foundations of creation. For more on these lines, and on vengeance and the related value of heroism, see notes to the introduction, as well as entries on "Vengeance" in the *Encyclopaedia Judaica* and on "Heroism" in *Contemporary Jewish Religious Thought* by Yeshayahu Leibowitz (1987, pp. 363–70); both sources make clear the rabbinic position that removes vengeance from the flawed human plane, reserving it for God and specifying that overcoming the desire for revenge constitutes part of the heroic character in the rabbinic context. In a notable and haunting echo of "On the Slaughter," some two decades after the publication of the poem, Leib Jaffe, the editor of the first daily Hebrew paper in Palestine, *Haaretz*, responded to rumors that young Jews seeking revenge for the recent murder of Jewish settlers had killed an innocent young Palestinian Arab: "The shedding of innocent blood shakes the foundations of the world. On land soaked with innocent blood, nothing will sprout, our nation's freedom will not arise, and its future will not bloom" (Zipperstein, 1993, p. 319).

Early Work (1890—1899)

I'd stand: Bialik, *Letters*, vol. I (1938), p. 167.

TO THE BIRD (אל-הציפור)

With its publication in 1892, when he was nineteen, this poem established Bialik as *the* rising star in Hebrew literary circles. It went through numerous drafts and full-fledged versions, and its appeal was such that parts of the poem were circulated in manuscript and memorized by his classmates at the Volozhin yeshiva. The subtly constructed voice of the poem's "young-old" speaker represents Bialik himself, but also the aspiring poet's generation as a whole and the historical people of Israel. For all of its Romantic, Orientalizing, and even adolescent envisioning of a distant, dreamed-of land, the poem impresses with its sweep and anticipation of the young poet's developed capacity for folding pockets of psychological and even ideological complication into his poetry. As a student at Volozhin, he became a member of Netzah Yisrael, a secret society whose manifesto called for support of both "the idea of 'settlement' (in the Holy Land)...in accordance with our faith and national aspirations, and the improvement of the moral conduct of those among our co-religionists who settle in our sacred land." While that mention of "moral conduct" remained vague, Bialik's cultural hero and mentor, Ahad Ha'Am, was—early on (in his essay "Truth from Eretz Israel," 1891) and then again twenty years later after accelerated Jewish immigration—outspoken about the treatment of the

Arabs living in Palestine by Jewish settlers at the time (Zipperstein, 1993, pp. 199–200). (Arabs, it should be noted, do not appear as part of the Palestinian landscape in the teenage Bialik's poem.) Ahad Ha'Am also wrote to the writer/farmer Moshe Smilansky in 1913: "If Palestinian Jewry is unable to exercise restraint and decency now that it holds little power, how much worse will it be when we control the land and its Arab inhabitants" (Zipperstein, 1993, pp. 246–47). His strongest statement on the ethical underpinnings of the Jewish claim to a presence in Palestine, let alone self-determinacy there, came in a 1922 letter: *"Our blood was spilled like water in every corner of the world for thousands of years, but we did not spill blood.* We always remembered that the great ethical teachings that our ancestors bequeathed us were the teachings of the future . . . . For without these principles . . . what are we, and what will be our life in this land?" (See note to "On the Slaughter" above, and Zipperstein, 1993, pp. 246–48 and 319–21.) Bialik himself rarely addressed the "Arab–Jewish question" directly. (His talk called "Eretz Yisrael" [The Land of Israel], delivered in 1929 or 1930, is one notable, if also condescending, exception: "There is in the Land of Israel sufficient room for two peoples. We do not want to push the Arabs from the land. We do not say, 'Let's expel them to the desert,' like Abraham the Patriarch did in his day to his son Ishmael. . . . We've come to expel the desert from the land.") By the same token, he embraced and promoted the genius of Hebrew poetry from Muslim Spain but was largely uninformed when it came to the Arabic (and Judeo-Arabic) heritage from which it derived. It's worth noting—especially given the ways in which Bialik's reputation developed over the course of the following century and a quarter, and down to this moment—that Benjamin Harshav calls "To the Bird" "both the first national [Hebrew] poem and Bialik's last Zionist poem" (2014, p. 129).

MY RETURN (בתשובתי)

Bialik dated this poem to 1891, though documentary evidence points convincingly to 1896 or 1897 as the more likely date of composition. Apart from its autobiographical relevance (the poem treats what seems to be the poet's actual return to his grandparents' home, from the yeshiva and his stay in Odessa), the title also encodes in caustic fashion associations with *teshuva* (religious penitence, or "return").

A SUMMER DAY (ביום קיץ, יום חום)

Initially untitled, perhaps because in fact the poem is not about summer at all but, like so many of Bialik's best poems, about a complex evolution of feeling and grasp of relation. It shows the young poet maturing into his signature style at every level. On journal publication, it was widely praised and embraced by the most sophisticated of Hebrew's younger high-modernist writers—Y. H. Brenner and Uri Nisan Gnessin—who (as Brenner tells it) memorized it and recited it aloud to one another with great enthusiasm.

AND THE PEOPLE ARE GRASS (אכן חציר העם)

This is the first of his poems in which Bialik takes on a prophetic stance and tone. The poem responds most immediately to the preparations for the First Zionist Congress of 1897 and, echoing Isaiah, expresses rage at both communal leaders and the apathetic Jewish communities of Europe. Following Ahad Ha'Am, Bialik implicitly argues that the primary problem with Jewish life in the Pale was psychological rather than religious, economic, or political. He objected to Herzl's "assimilated" and instrumental Zionism, which sought the immediate establishment of a Jewish state in the Land of Israel. "Ahad Ha'am spoke of the calcification of the Jewish heart," writes Dan Miron, "the loss of living feeling behind the law written in the books. Bialik speaks of drying, loss of softness and suppleness" (*Songs*, 2000).

MIDNIGHT PRAYER (תיקון חצות)

The Hebrew title is "Tikkun Hatzot"—literally, "Midnight Repair." *Tikkun* here involves a spiritual rectification, one that in the traditional Jewish context involves rising in the middle of the night to engage in intensive prayer sessions. In a letter to Ahad Ha'Am, who edited the journal where this poem was first published, Bialik expressed his surprise at his mentor's attraction to the poem for its bitter irony, which the editor read as a tacit critique of traditional culture's failure to correct its own course in the real world. The thrust of the poem isn't subtle irony, responded the twenty-five-year-old poet, so much as "true feeling...a silent sigh in the face of absolute barrenness and utter despair." See Orlan (1971), p. 60.

OVER YOUR HEART (על לבבכם ששמם)

The referent of this semi-expressionistic poem's central second-person pronoun seems to float in the cultural air, and the subject is at once sharply defined and ambiguous. Does Bialik have in mind the political Zionists of the moment, for whom he had a hard time concealing his contempt? (See "The Word.") Or is the poem a critique of a certain public or institutional layer of the organized Jewish community more generally? Or of a particular and specious literary or journalistic faction? Or of himself? All of the above? Whatever the case, the crisis runs deep. The opening line of the Hebrew explicitly mentions the "invalid mezuzah" on the ruins of the heart. Placed on doorposts in Jewish homes and other buildings, the small parchment scroll held in its case contains the central prayer of the liturgy, the Shema, and has to be written and maintained in a prescribed ritual manner in order to remain "valid," so as to fulfill the commandment to post them and thereby bless the home to ward off evil. When it's no longer properly made and attached to the doorpost, demons take root between the walls (of the home or heart). The word I've translated as "desolation" in line 12 (*shimmamon*) is sometimes used in Hebrew poems of the day to translate Baudelaire's *ennui* (see Hamutal Bar Yosef, "Bialik and the Baudelairian Triangle: Ennui, Cats and Spider Webs," *Jewish Studies Quarterly* 1, no. 4 [1993/94], p. 370, and note to "When the Days Grow Long," below). In Ezekiel 4:16, it's understood as "desperation," "despair," "terror," or "horror."

The Middle Years: Part I *(1900–1903)*

Here can be found: Zipperstein, *The Jews of Odessa: A Cultural History, 1794–1881* (1985), p. 26.

Seven miles around Odessa: Zipperstein (1985), pp. 1 and 48.

ZEPHYRS (צפרירים)

Bialik's move to Odessa in 1900 brought with it a major shift in mood: darkness to light is how it's often described, and "Zephyrs" is the first important poem he wrote in the place that would become his home for the next two decades. Bialik's "zephyrs" are creatures or spirits for which he adopted the Hebrew term *tzafririm* (derived from the Aramaic for morning, *tzafra*). He initially defined *tzafririm* as "morning spirits, according to the Kabbalists," though he was clearly drawing on a rich tradition of sprite-like and even demonic figures that appear in Russian literature and western mythology. In this poem, they're associated with a polymorphous erotic awakening, one that extends from the natural world (of light and air) into the body and the innermost self and selflessness.

Lines 35, 49: Psalms 69:2: "I am come unto deep waters where floods overflow me."

I SCATTERED MY SIGHS (זריתי לרוח אנחתי)

While the poem makes perfect figurative sense on the surface level, biblical allusions complicate the associative field in two different prophetic directions. The image of scattering to the wind, from Ezekiel 5:1–2, brings out overtones of the prophet's warning to the people about their dissolute behavior: "And you, son of man, take a sharp sword...as a barber's razor, and pass *it* over your head and your beard; then take scales to weigh and divide the hair....One-third you shall scatter in the wind." The image of the blood and fire in Isaiah 9:5 carries overtones of messianic hope that serve as contrapuntal coloration of the despair implied by the image in the final line of Bialik's poem: "And garments rolled in blood will be used for burning and fuel of fire." There is also an echo of Ezekiel 16:6 ("wallowing in the blood"), which contrasts with Bialik's use of the same image in line 24 of "On the Slaughter." The opening of the poem recalls one of Bialik's early essays on *kinus*: "[T]he sons, if they wish to avoid being scattered in the world's wind, must turn and turn this earth, must plough and harrow it again and again... and if there is no tradition and chain of transmission in a literature—there can be no enlargement and development, and no renewal" ("The Hebrew Book"). See Moss (2009), p. 106ff. on this and the resistance to Bialik's thinking at the time.

STARS GLISTEN AND FADE (כוכבים מציצים וכבים)

Lines 11-12: Ecclesiastes 1:8, "All things are wearisome" ("full of weariness and labor"); Ecclesiastes 1:5–6: "The sun also rises, and the sun goes down, and hastens to the place where it arose.... The wind goes toward the south, and turns about to the north; it whirls about continually, and the wind returns again according to its circuits."

ONLY A LINE OF SUNLIGHT (רק קו שמש אחד)

Again, the lurking presence of the floating or ambiguous referent, as what seems to be a poem about the male speaker's intense encounter with female sexuality has also been read as a poem about his soul (which is gendered feminine in Hebrew and very much part of an erotic dynamic in the history of Hebrew poetry and liturgy). In this latter scheme, the speaker is repulsed by his own attraction to the new world of secular learning and living, beyond the traditional Jewish world he has left behind. However one reads it, the poem is ripeness itself, even over-ripeness, and the surface textures and tension of the Hebrew embody that feeling. Homonymic slippage contributes to the chromatic dimension of the verse. The first two words of the poem, for example—*rak kav* (only a line)—can be heard as *rakav* ("rotted"); in the translation, "only a line" yields "only align" (with echoes of E. M. Forster's "only connect").

THE SEA OF SILENCE SPITS OUT SECRETS (ים הדממה פולט סודות)

Line 1: As with "Only a Line of Sunlight," the sound matrix of the Hebrew here blurs and yields an interesting subliminal reading. Zali Gurevitch points out (2018, p. 18) that when one reads the poem in Bialik's Ashkenazic pronunciation, with its falling stresses, it sounds like *YAma de-Mamma*: the sea of mother—as the poem itself and its rhythms promise protection and threaten suffocation. Its secret recalls Dryden's comment about what is "secretly in the poet" (see the introduction to this volume, p. xxviii). By contrast, the emphatic rising stress of the Sephardic pronunciation with which the overwhelming majority of speakers of Hebrew read Bialik today yields *YAM ha-dmaMAH*: the sea of silence. This one example illustrates how very different the effect of the two systems of pronunciation are, when it comes to primary elements such as rhythm and overall feel, and why it is that this shift in pronunciation and linguistic context contributed to Bialik's eventual silence and sense of his own obsolescence as a poet once he settled in Tel Aviv. For more on the difference between Ashkenazic and Sephardic pronunciation, or dialects, and on the various subdialects within the world of Ashkenazic pronunciation, see Harshav (1993), pp. 153–66. The debate over which system should be used in the modern Hebrew revival was hotly contested on the political (and not only cultural) level. See Bialik's essay "Culture and Politics" (1935) and more on this in Moss (2009), pp. 81–82 and 96–97.

ALONE (לבדי)

A classic instance of the speaker being caught between the two worlds that run through so much of his work—on the one hand, the old world of traditional study, and on the other, the modernity that was drawing him and his peers outward. See notes to "I Scattered My Sighs to the Wind," and also Moss (2009), pp. 108–09. The complicated locus of "song" and "new song" is an abiding subject for Bialik. Both come across as an outside presence that called to those who have already abandoned the house of study and its indwelling presence. And yet, that very notion of "new song" is what the tradition itself calls for—repeatedly in Scripture, and especially in Psalms 96:1: "Sing to the Lord a new song, sing to the Lord, all the earth." We also find it front and center in rabbinic literature: "Every day, ministering angels are created from the fiery stream, and utter song, and cease to be" (Talmud, *Hagigah* 14a); and, "As new water flows from the well each hour, so Israel renews its song" (*Midrash Tehillim* 87:7). Likewise, it runs up through late Antiquity and into the Middle Ages: "If not for the poetry and song that the creatures of flesh and blood proclaim before me each day, I would not have created my world" (*Alfa beita de-Rabbi Aqiva*, version 1, *Battei Midrashot*, 2:343–44), and more.

We find a curious modern instantiation of the notion of "new song" in the writings of Naftali Zvi Yehuda Berlin (1816-1893), known as the Netziv, who directed the Volozhin Yeshiva for many years, including the period when Bialik was a student there. In a commentary on the Torah that is based on his teachings of the weekly Torah portion at Volozhin, Berlin writes: "In *Nedarim* 38a, it is suggested that the word *shira*, as in 'Write down this *shira* [song]' [Deuteronomy 31:19—the 'Song of Moses'], applies to the entire Torah.... We must suggest that Torah as a whole contains the inner qualities of poetry, in that poetry uses language in a unique way. Everyone knows that poetry differs from prose in that the ideas are not explicitly expressed, as in prose. In poetry, one needs a commentary alongside the poem to say, 'This stanza refers to this or that.' This is not an external addition to the text, but this is the very nature of poetry, even for the layman. Such is the nature of Torah" (The Netziv, *HaEmek Davar*, introduction to Torah, 3, Sefaria website). Compare this with Bialik's description of the difference between poetry and prose in "Revealment and Concealment" (2000), pp. 24–25 (see note to "He Gazed and Died," below). The "ancient lament" at the end of the poem alludes to the genre of the lament itself but specifically calls to mind the Book of Lamentations and the fall of

Jerusalem and the Temple, as well as other poems and prayers com-
memorating that event and similar crises in the people's history.

I DIDN'T WIN LIGHT IN A WINDFALL (לא זכיתי באור מן-ההפקר)

One of the most famous poems in the Bialikian canon, a taut,
charged, and aggressively ambiguous expression of the poet's task
and achievement, in which Romantic impulses meet a harder-core
economic understanding of poetry as labor and complex ownership
and exchange. The poem's undertow also gives powerful voice to his
horror at the vulgarization his poetry is subject to once it's out of his
hands (and heart). Also central to this dynamic is a less-than-pious
but religious economy of sacrifice, one in which—as poet Dahlia
Ravikovitch has noted—poetry itself (rather than the law) punishes
the poet for the fire he sets in people's hearts (Orlan, p. 100). The
final lines of the poem allude to Isaiah and Exodus: Isaiah 50:11:
"Behold, all ye that kindle a fire, that compass yourselves about
with sparks: walk in the light of your fire, and in the sparks that ye
have kindled. This shall ye have of mine hand; ye shall lie down in
sorrow"; Ezekiel 44:15: "But the priests, the Levites ... shall stand
before me to offer unto me the fat and the blood, says the Lord
God"; Exodus 22:6: "If fire break out, and catch in thorns, so that
the stacks of corn, or the standing corn, or the field, be consumed
therewith; he that kindled the fire shall surely make restitution."
See Bialik's "Halakhah and Aggadah" for interesting parallels to
this poem, especially: "Real art, ... like the Torah, cannot be truly
served except by him who sacrifices his life for it—in order to give
life. What matters is the vital relation of the artist to the form of
life which lies before him. If an artist disqualifies any form of life
as unsuitable for art, the question at once arises whether it is not
he himself who is unqualified in that particular regard. But can we
draw living water from this rock of *halakhah* [the body of literature
treating religious law and practice]? ... Yes, if you have the divine
rod in your hand and the fountain of life in your heart. If we had true
artists and inspired creators ... they would draw speech even out of
this rock." See *Revealment and Concealment* (2000), pp. 79–80.

NEWS (בשורה)

The second section of the poem in the original. Equal parts grounded lyric and soaring concept (one leading into the other and back), the poem is in many ways a classic echo of the metaphysical Andalusian poetry of Solomon Ibn Gabirol, the Andalusian Hebrew poet to whom Bialik was most deeply—and some would say obsessively—drawn. See, for instance, "The Garden," in *Selected Poems of Solomon Ibn Gabirol*, translation by Peter Cole (2001), p. 67. As in so many of Ibn Gabirol's liturgical and nonliturgical poems (and in the Hebrew literary tradition as a whole), here, too, the renewal of song is central.

CITY OF SLAUGHTER (בעיר ההרגה)

The Hebrew title is, literally, "In the City of Slaughter" (or "Killing"). See introduction and notes there for detailed background to the poem. Its journal publication was delayed by three months of negotiations with the government censor in St. Petersburg. The censor—a Jewish convert to Christianity—objected not to the social and political ramifications of the poem but to its theology: He considered the poem's depiction of God to be blasphemous. As a result, the poem was first published with changes to a number of lines and under the more obscure and distantly historical title "The Burden [Prophecy] of Nemirov," employing the biblical word for "prophecy" (*masa*) and alluding to the name of a village in Poland where a far worse massacre of Jews occurred in 1648 (killing between three and six thousand), during what has become known as the Khmelnitzky uprising. The death toll among Ukrainian Jews that year and the next came to some twenty thousand.

The twelve stanzas of the poem take us through the course of a full day during which the narrator (God, as it eventually becomes clear) has the poet-prophet survey the scene of the slaughter. The opening line of the Hebrew establishes the direct link to the blunt opening of the Book of Jonah 1:2, where God orders Jonah to "Get up and go to the great city of Nineveh." It also enfolds overtones of the command to Abraham in Genesis 12:1 to "Go from your country." The end of the poem employs a similar formulation, alluding to Amos 7:12: "Go, seer, flee to the land of Judah." Jeremiah, Isaiah, and others are echoed throughout. Ezekiel is especially prominent—for one, with the recurring employment of the address to the poet-witness as "Son of Man" (the term with which Ezekiel is addressed by God some ninety-three times—see also notes to "I Scattered My Sighs" in this volume) and also with the reference to "wheels within wheels." Almost all of these and the many other obvious and less obvious allusions to Scripture violently rotate the biblical reference on its axis and turn the tradition against itself and its God.

In the wake of the pogrom and all the publicity around it, and especially after the publication and widespread dissemination of the poem, calls for Jewish self-defense spread widely and took root—for better and for worse. And this, too, involved some of that strangeness of the lives led by political poems. Bialik's translator, Jabotin-sky, became one of the leading figures in the call to arms, and—whether or not one considers this a responsible or even valid reading of the poem—there is arguably a direct line from "City of Slaughter" to the formation of Jewish underground resistance brigades in the Pale and in British Mandate Palestine, to the establishment of the State of Israel in 1948, and on to the IDF and some of the worst settler violence on the West Bank and in Gaza today. Michael Stanislawski points out how deeply this involves a basic failure to understand Bialik's poem: Jabotinsky's Russian version, he said, amounted to a systematic "de-Judaization of its entire symbolic and semiotic system." Jabotinsky "succeeded most strikingly in subverting the highly subversive ideational core of Bialik's original" (pp. 191–92). Instead, the grotesque but effective misreading articulated in his 1924 introduction to an English edition of Bialik's poems renders the poet as "a singer of triumphant, invisible Manhood, of the arm that wields the sword, of muscles of granite and sinews of steel" (p. 194).

On the line of descent from Jabotinsky's translation of the poem to the IDF of today, see, for instance, Yonatan Toubal in *Haaretz*, October 27, 2022; also Or Kashti and Gili Izikovitch on the use of Bialik's poem by IDF troops in the current Gaza war, in *Haaretz*, March 26, 2024, and Anita Shapira, "'In the City of Slaughter' vs. 'He Told Her'" (*Prooftexts* 25 [2005]), pp. 97-98, 101, on the ways in which Bialik's call for awakening was *not* a call to arms. Shapira notes that, despite the Jewish specificity of this poem, it is the most universal of his poems of wrath, the most local proving to have the broadest reach—well beyond the particulars of Russian or any other Jewry. Bialik's notes for the commissioned report—which he never released—were, only some ninety years later, published as *Testimonies of the Victims of the Kishinev Pogrom: As Assembled by Hayim Nahman Bialik et al.*, edited by Yaakov Goren (1991, Hebrew); see also Mikhal Dekel, "'From the Mouth of the Raped Woman Rivka Schiff,' Kishinev, 1903," in *WSQ: Women's Studies Quarterly* 36, no.1 (2008). Building on psychoanalytic and political-theological critiques of the poem by Gluzman, Hever, and Miron (2005), Dekel's feminist reading understands Bialik's suppression of the "objective" documentary material and his turn to the more subjective lyrical-prophetic mode as being rooted in both the poet's own experience of humiliating trauma and abuse as a child and in a Romantic-Zionist distancing and shift of perspective. For an updated reading of the poem's powerful undertow, a reading that runs contrary to the mainstream and muscular Jabotinskian line, see Gideon Levy, "Khan Yunis, Gaza's City of Slaughter," *Haaretz*, April 20, 2025.

It's worth noting as well the parallel track of Bialik's engagement during this fulcral moment. While he was conducting the research in Kishinev, he was, during the evening, writing a detailed autobiographical sketch at the request of editor Joseph Klausner. With the publication of "City of Slaughter," he would, at age thirty, become widely regarded as the "poet of the national renaissance" (the term was first used by Joseph Klausner after the 1901 publication of

Bialik's first volume of poems). Although Bialik never produced the prose of his delegation's report, he did—instead—compose a prose "memoir." See Penkower (2006).

The Middle Years, Part II (1903–1916)

Odessa encouraged: Fichman, in Cole, *Hebrew Writers on Writing* (2008), p. 46.

As for my impressions of Warsaw: letter to Ravnitzky on December 28, 1901, in Bialik, *Letters*, vol. I, p. 196.

FROM "WINTER SONGS" (משירי החורף)

Between 1901 and 1903, Bialik wrote two series of "winter songs" consisting of six or seven discrete poems. This is the first of the 1903 series and was written in December, which is to say, only a few months after he'd finished "City of Slaughter."

Line 11: Numbers 17:8: "And it came to pass, that on the morrow Moses went into the tabernacle of witness; and, behold, the rod of Aaron for the house of Levi was budded, and brought forth buds, and bloomed blossoms"; Ezekiel 7:10: "Behold the day, behold, it is come: the morning is gone forth; the rod hath blossomed, pride hath budded."

THE WORD (דבר)

The title might also be translated as "Speech" or "Burden." Bialik's first neo-prophetic poem written in free verse, it was composed some two months after Herzl's death in the summer of 1904. The younger Bialik had greeted Herzl's appearance on the scene with something far more blatantly parodic, a poem in which he'd called a Herzl-like figure "Rabbi Zarach" and saw him in a line of Jewish false Messiahs (see Miron, *Collected Poems: 1890–1898*, pp. 320–22). "The Word" emerged directly out of the welter of arguments within the Zionist movement over how best to respond to the challenge facing the Jewish communities of Europe and the world at the time.

Bialik and others were particularly upset by Herzl's endorsement of a British plan, put forth several months after the pogrom at Kishinev, to establish a "protectorate" for the Jewish people in Uganda. (This after Herzl himself had proposed several other non-Palestinian options for a Jewish homeland, including Cyprus or the Sinai Peninsula.) As with most arguments pertaining to Zionism, Bialik took the position of Ahad Ha'am, his mentor, who stressed a more moderate and "spiritual Zionism" over Herzl's purely political vision. The people (not God) address their prophet in this poem—though opinions have been divided as to who this prophet figure is: Herzl? Bialik himself (objecting to the reduction of his work to a position he didn't hold)? As we see again and again, this is exactly one of the strengths of Bialik's poetry—that it reacts so powerfully with so much around it and, as a result, lends itself to intensifying engagement in numerous and surprising ways. Aberbach points out that, at the exact midpoint of the poem, we encounter the grave dug by the people for itself, and with a hoe or shovel forged by the prophet. The opening line alludes to Isaiah 6:6—"Then flew one of the seraphim unto me, having a live coal in his hand, which he had taken with the tongs from off the altar"—and to Numbers 16:37: "And the Lord spoke to Moses, saying:... Speak to Eleazar, the son of Aaron the priest, and tell him to take up the fire-pans out of the burnings and scatter thou the fire yonder." In short, the prophet's word is among us; the question is how to apply it.

AND IF THE ANGEL ASKS (ואם-ישאל המלאך)

As is often the case, Bialik strings a series of radically repurposed biblical phrases through the poem, moving from Job's Satan "going to and fro in the earth" to 1 Kings' "little cloud out of the sea, like a man's hand"; from the Song of Songs to Lamentations; and more. He is also working from popular superstitions and, possibly, a Yiddish story, "Three Gifts," by I. L. Peretz, who was one of Bialik's literary heroes. (Bialik's poem was composed not long after the story was published.) As the speaker in the poem responds to a series of questions that the angel asks about his soul, he touches on what Bialik's early biographer Fischel Lachover calls "the deep truth about his poetry, that it brought back to life with its creative spirit the dead letters of Hebrew, as on his grandfather's bookshelf the dead of the world were shaken." "And If the Angel Asks" picks up in many ways on one of Bialik's earliest poems, "The Angel," which is based on his reading of Lermontov: "That angel soaring on high / and bearing a soul on his arm— / stars, the heavenly hosts, / lend an ear to his song."

The "love" that the speaker seeks in the poem tells us a good deal about Bialik's otherwise "happy" marriage to Manya, but there is of course more to it than that. While in Kishinev on his fact-finding mission, Bialik met a painter who went by the name Ira Jan (her real name was Esphir or Esther Yoselevitch), and they began an intense relationship of an ambiguous sort that lasted for several years. She left her husband and later wrote about the period: "These three weeks gave me the happiness of being with our great poet. He brought me back to my people and to myself" (https://en.wikipedia.org/wiki/Ira_Jan#cite_note-lyukimson-3). Bialik eventually broke off the relationship, and Jan immigrated to Tel Aviv. According to some accounts, she hovers in the background of numerous poems of his. She also translated some of his work into Russian.

FROM "THE POOL" (הבריכה)

One of Bialik's most famous poems, "The Pool" was begun in Warsaw in 1904 and finished in Odessa the following summer. The excerpt translated here, which brings the poem to a close, appears to have been composed in a single sitting in Odessa. Bialik's obsession with dualities in tension becomes an essential part of the free-verse poem's subject. This is Bialik's most Wordsworthian poem (though it isn't clear that this belated Wordsworthian poet was at all familiar with Wordsworth's poetry). The centrality of "reflection" in the poem also suggests a Kabbalistic mythopoetic framework. Others have read the poem as a model of translation and its quasi-magical powers to contain things greater than itself.

BRING ME IN UNDER YOUR WING (הכניסיני תחת כנפך)

While this poem is clearly a personal lyric, and very possibly ad-
dressed to a single, specific individual, its imagery—the wing, the
covering (alluding to Ruth and Ezekiel and the concealment of na-
kedness), and the dramatic situation of the work—evokes a world
of highly suggestive religious and Kabbalistic associations. Con-
sciously or unconsciously, the poem becomes, in part, a statement
about the state of the soul, and especially the Jewish soul, within a
secular world. It was written after Bialik's return home to Odessa
(and his wife) from a long period of travel in 1905. Bialik, notes
Fichman, felt that the poem—carrying over the poetics of War-
saw—opened up a new lyric line for him (1946, p. 346). The "un-
wanted" prayers of lines 4 and 20 (in the slippery Hebrew, "rejected"
or "neglected") highlight the poem's chronic liminality—a longing
that runs deep but finds no answer. The circular structure returns
us to the speaker's unwanted prayers as it underscores his exile
from oneness and, to an extent, from language. At the same time,
the verbal structure itself conveys a sense of rest and closure, even
as the poem tells of a denial of consolation and a painful suspension
between worlds. Among the poet's signature works.

FROM "SCROLL OF FIRE" (מגלת האש)

An excerpt from what Miron calls "the most encompassing, com-
plex, and problematic of Bialik's poems." Bialik's own and much
later analysis of this quasi-epic symbolist poem suggests, say many,
that he himself didn't quite understand what he'd done, or was still
struggling with it, especially in the later parts of the poem (not
translated here). It is clear, however, that his primary aim in "Scroll
of Fire" was to create a poem around the rabbinic legend of the
"eternal light" that was saved from the destruction of the Jerusa-
lem Temple and hidden (ganuz), initially outside of Jerusalem and
eventually in Diasporic exile, to ensure its survival for generations
to come. The work's prose-poem form derives in part from what
he'd been reading in Russian (and French in Russian translation). It
was written in Odessa, in early summer, in the thick of the unrest

of the day and not long after the late-June mutiny on the battleship *Potemkin*, which resulted in the shelling of the city itself. Bialik and thousands of others fled to a forest above the city and watched the scene unfold through the night, as oil tanks burst into flame and exploded, setting off massive fires.

The passage translated here is from the opening of the nine-part poem. The "Glory" of the final sentence of the excerpt renders the Hebrew word "Shekhinah." The poem is saturated with biblical allusion, to Isaiah, Psalms, Ezekiel, Exodus, and more. Fichman calls it "a midrash of a generation, questioning its path" at a critical moment of intense pressure and volatility. It is, he adds, not an allegory of the Russian Revolution, but a poem about the mystery of Jewish existence, its ongoing struggle for its soul and survival, and the kind of internal power that has, historically, been behind that survival.

SUMMER DIES (הקיץ גווע)

Poet Natan Zach calls this "quintessentially Bialikian, one of his most beautiful and most perfect poems....The landscape is bare and a person stands alone in the emptying distance" (Orlan, p. 130). While it comes across as a kind of art for art's sake word painting, the underlying structure charges it with something more, which is invoked in the most nuanced and complex of fashions—through the web of allusions, and especially in the textures and tensions of the verse itself. In other words, the residue of deep cultural and even organic translation is, compositionally speaking, everywhere in these twelve lines, and the mood and cast of which shifts from celebration to melancholy, richness to subsistence, grandeur to loneness and even bleakness. Apart from the biblical allusions to Ezekiel (the same passage from chapter 16 that "On the Slaughter" echoes) and to the famous lines in Psalm 121 ("I lift my eyes to the hills, whence cometh my help"), the quiet incorporation of a passage from the Mishnaic Tractate *Shabbat* (2:7) deepens the timbre of the whole: "There are three things a person must say in his home on the Sabbath evening as the darkness falls: Have you tithed?

Have you marked the boundary? Did you light the candle[s]?"
While a quiet irony hovers near this closing gesture, and some have
read it as parodic, the poem is at once subtler, bleaker, and in its
stark way more beautiful and ominous than parody of the Talmu-
dic passage might imply.

I KNEW ON A NIGHT OF THICK DARKNESS (ידעתי בליל ערפל)

This poem was first published as part of a Bialikian chapbook
called *Poems of Wrath*, which included reprintings of "On the
Slaughter" and "City of Slaughter" and was released in response to
the proliferation of anti-Jewish violence that took place in Russia
during the 1905 revolution. On October 26, Bialik wrote to a friend
about the worst of the pogroms, which occurred in Odessa, noting
how the reports in the international press didn't begin to convey
the reality of the situation: "They finished burying the victims to-
day—over 300 Jews dead. More than 600 of the hooligans were
killed. Tremendous destruction. Some 20,000 are left without
clothing or shelter.... The army and police joined forces with the
hooligans in the rioting and the killing. If not for our courageous
defenders, we'd have all been lost" (*Letters*, vol. II, October 26,
1905). A poet-prophet addresses the people, and his indictment
drifts at once inward toward the Jewish community (and its God)
and outward to the apathetic world at large—though all this occurs
under the sign of a striking ambiguity. Miron calls this "the most
riddling and allusive of Bialik's prophetic poems, a cosmic picture
of awesome power is drawn as well as one of dissolution and end-
ing" (*Songs of Bialik*, 2000). Some have seen the poem as Bialik's
reaction against himself for having blamed the victims at Kishinev.
See Bar Yosef, "Bialik and the Russian Revolutions," pp. 7–9. The
title draws on Joel 2:2, among other biblical passages: "A day of
darkness and gloom, a day of clouds and thick darkness...nothing
like it has ever happened," and the final image alludes to Leviticus
26:25: "I [God] will bring a sword against you to wreak vengeance
for the Covenant." As in "On the Slaughter," images of the desire
for vengeance are tempered by the poem's ambiguities—ironies

blending with realities and allegorical imagery giving way to powerful, elemental feeling. "Even if [God] wakes from his indifference," writes Miron, "and comes out with his great sword, his arm is broken and his heart pierced, and he carries with him not only weakness but also shame ('a mark of failure on the broken arm of God'). The people is trampled and robbed, drowning in its agony and doomed to see how the false 'redemption of the world' (Socialism) celebrates its victory over the graves of its dead."

DUSK (עַרְבִית)

A characteristic blurring of personal and national mood gives expression to Bialik's despair: on the one hand, disgust with himself and his poetry, and perhaps also with the absence of a female presence (the Hebrew of line two can refer either to the sun—"it"—or to a "her" who hasn't been in touch); on the other hand, his anger at both his own community and the communities that have been threatening and assaulting Russian Jewry in a series of pogroms over the course of three difficult years (1903–06). In Odessa alone, estimates put the total number of deaths in violence surrounding the 1905 Revolution at five hundred, with over three thousand injured (Zipperstein, 1993, p. 222). A few months before he composed this poem, Bialik wrote to a friend and mentioned being in the grip of "something like a feeling of numbness and dullness at heart, I can't pick up a pen, my private life has no scent or taste to it…and sometimes a mood comes over me in which I want to end it all— but I'm too lazy to do the right thing. I don't have the strength for that either…and in the end, it's all vanity. Scum and pettiness— that's my share" (Bialik, *Letters*, vol. II, p. 45). That August, he wrote his wife from the Zionist Congress at the Hague and described the gathering as a waste of time: "I left with a heavy heart and broken spirit. I didn't even have the strength to weep" (Bialik, *Letters*, vol. II, p. 59). In a lecture Bialik gave several months earlier, "Our Young Poetry," he talked about how the "sunset" of the national poetry had come, and it should "fold up its prayer shawl, go home to say its evening prayers alone," i.e., to make way for the new poetry of personal lyricism that begins in the heart of the individual Jew and comes back to it. In the penultimate stanza, the "evening of idiot confusion" is a loaded term in the Hebrew (*tumtum*), the Talmudic roots of which refer to a person of indeterminate gender (and the etymology of which points to something "hidden"; it also yields the word for "idiot" or "stupid"). The Satanic figure of the last stanza is, in the Hebrew, Ashmedai, King of Demons, who, in the Talmud, is associated with Solomon and verses from the Book of Ecclesiastes (see *The Book of Legends*, edited by Bialik and Ravnitzky, 1992, pp. 123:107 and 129:122).

AND WHEN DAYS GROW LONG (והיה כי יארכו הימים)

Critics have generally read this free-verse poem in the context of the language wars of the day and the Czernowitz Yiddish Conference's 1908 plan to declare Yiddish a national Jewish language. The central debate was whether the declaration should read "*a* national language" or "*the* national language" (as opposed to Hebrew). It's worth noting that Herzl's utopian novel, *Altneuland* (*The Old New Land*), doesn't specify what language is spoken on the envisioned country's streets, but it clearly isn't Hebrew or Yiddish. Some have seen this poem as at least in part a "satiric" or even "cruelly parodic" reaction against the conference-goers and their statement. That said, Yiddish was Bialik's mother tongue and his primary spoken language, and he occasionally wrote in it. As with some of his earlier poems ("Only a Line of Sunlight" and even "My Return"), the language of decadence enters in from European literature, with its emphasis on ennui, which in the Hebrew becomes "*shimmamon*," a complex sensation that reaches to the root of Bialik's larger vision of cultural revival (see note to "Over Your Heart"). The poem takes up a much broader dimension of Jewish and other longing than the one at the heart of the Yiddish revival. While Bialik was a great believer in the revival of spoken Hebrew and the importance of writing in Hebrew, he admitted that it was far easier for him to write of the intimacies of childhood and his deepest feeling through Yiddish (see Feinstein, pp. 250–52). The poem's title draws on Ezekiel 12:22: "Son of man, what is this proverb that you people have in the land of Israel, which says, 'The days grow long [or: many], and every vision fails'?" This, in other words, is the great culmination of the storied messianic longing and waiting (however that longing is understood): a yawn and perhaps amused observance of self-delusion that itself somehow maintains the tradition even as it's used here to undermine it.

BEFORE THE BOOKSHELF (לפני ארון הספרים)

The context makes it clear that this is a collection of traditional Hebrew books, as one would normally find in a *beit midrash* or house of study. Bialik wrote this poem immediately after completing a massive project of selecting, editing, and "translating" rabbinic legends (from ancient Hebrew and Aramaic into modern Hebrew) for a compendium called *Sefer HaAggadah* (*The Book of Legends*). The collection constitutes the imaginative history of classical rabbinic Judaism and in many ways the subconscious of Jewish literature. As usual, Bialik's partner in this enterprise was Yehoshua Ravnitzky, and the result of their labor was a book that has served several generations of readers seeking to make their way back to the world of traditional Jewish envisioning without having to enter institutional religious settings. The learning they poured into their synthetic work is staggering; the labor itself took up much of Bialik's energies in the late 1900s. But a lifetime of compounded study and dreamwork went into it, and in many respects the broader project it was part of would occupy the rest of his life as well. Given the complex constitution and economy of Bialik's cultural ecosystem, it's perhaps not surprising that an elegiac and even harsh poem like "Before the Bookshelf" would follow the triumphant production of *The Book of Legends* (the English translation of which weighs in at 920 pages of small print set out in two columns per page). The poem reflects a kind of postpartum depression of a very deep sort, a recognition of the extent to which this poet of doubleness was doubly vulnerable and exposed. For one, the knowledge and spiritual legacy that gave rise to his poetry and all that mattered to him were rapidly becoming obsolete; and second, his best attempts to translate what he knew into an ongoing life in a new context were, he felt at some level of his self and soul, pointless. And yet, even as the poet felt that he no longer knew the languages he once was able to translate from, deep translation itself remained his lifelong calling. At this point, he was still answering that call.

As for his referring to himself in the poem as "the last of the last," see Simon Rawidowicz in "Israel: The Ever-Dying People": "And Bialik—did he not himself often surrender to the fear of being the last....It was this...that drove him to save the past, to recreate and refashion it....Whoever has not grasped this psychological background of Bialik's effort—his fear of the end and his struggle between end and beginning—cannot really understand his life, his conflicts, and his achievements" (in *State of Israel, Diaspora, and Jewish Continuity*, edited by Benjamin Ravid, 1986, p. 59). Also see Rawidowicz in "Israel: Ever-Dying": "He who studies Jewish history will readily discover that there was hardly a generation in the Diaspora period which did not consider itself the last link in Israel's chain" (ibid. p. 211). Also of serious interest are Rawidowicz's "Conversations with Bialik" (Hebrew), which were conducted when this maverick Polish-born thinker moved to Berlin in his mid-twenties and became close to Bialik before the latter left for Palestine.

A SMALL BRANCH SANK (צנח לו זלזל)

This poem constitutes an important marker of Bialik's "period of silence," the culmination of his dark poems of 1910–11 and what turned out to be a farewell of sorts to active composition of poetry for four years. He returned to the writing of poems later on, but only sporadically. Bialik was tortured by this block, which, he told Fichman, was "a kind of sickness, the nature of which I don't understand" (see Aberbach, 1988, p. 88; and Bialik, *Letters*, vol. II, p. 103). Brenner, characteristically, embraced the poem's bleakness: "It's good to pound one's head against the dark—to look into it with eyes wide open" (Orlan, 1971, p. 157).

The entire poem might be seen as a shadow-meditation on Psalms 1:3: "And he shall be like a tree planted by the rivers of water, that bringeth forth his fruit in his season; his leaf also shall not wither; and whatsoever he doeth shall prosper." Seasons count in this poem, which moves from autumn to winter and then spring. It's not irrelevant either, Aberbach notes, that Bialik wrote this poem around the time of his mother's death. She'd come to Odessa and lived with Bialik and his wife for a difficult final three years of her life.

HE GAZED AND DIED (הציץ ומת)

This poem grows from the ground of the famous Talmudic tale in *Hagigah* 14b, where four sages enter "the orchard" (*pardes*, which is later understood as the garden of fourfold interpretation—literal, homiletic, allegorical, and mystical; it's also, coincidentally, the name of the journal where Bialik's first poem was published). One of "the four," as they've become known in the tradition, Rabbi Ben Azzai, "gazed and died," meaning that the vision of the holy and its splendor was too much for him to bear. Another key text for understanding this poem is Bialik's best-known essay, "Revealment and Concealment in Language," which was completed in October 1915 (shortly before he composed "He Gazed and Died") and which ends with an allusion to those same sages who entered the *pardes*. Yet another expression of his dyadic consciousness, the essay treats the dual nature of human language to reveal mysteries even as it conceals them.

The image of the fifty gates at the opening is drawn from the Babylonian Talmud: "Fifty gates of understanding were created in the world, and they were all given, except for one" (*Rosh HaShanah* 21b). The poem comes to a close—which has been seen as either an opening out or an ultimate nullification—with the charged and elusive word *belimah* (literally, "without-what"). The mystical and quasi-scientific second- to eighth-century CE text, *Sefer Yetzirah* (the Book of Creation, or Formation), also has many gates running through it (beginning with the Talmudic gates of "understanding") and states that the world was created from the twenty-two letters of the Hebrew alphabet and the ten sephirot (or channels of divine consciousness). "Ten sephirot *belimah*" is how the Hebrew describes them, using a word that remains elusive and has generated worlds within worlds of commentary. The term first appears in Job 26:7: "He stretches out the north over empty space; he hangs the world on nothing [*belimah*]." Interpretations of Bialik's own use of the word in the poem have varied greatly, with many understanding it to mean "emptiness," a "void," "nothing," in the bleakest or simply existentialist sense. Others see a more generative "nothing" of the sort that we find in mystical literature. It has also been read as deriving from the root meaning "restraint." Here too we find Bialikian doubling, in which both positive and darker readings make perfect sense at one and the same time. In short, *belimah* embodies the problem of revelation: it locates what is beyond language within the realm of language itself. In a quietly powerful and disturbing manner, this algebraic "X"—equal parts utopian and dispiriting—brings us back to the beginning of Bialik's poetry and the cipher of the dreamed-of land in "To the Bird."

My choice to render *belimah* as "X" ("over the X of the deep") is based in part on what Bialik writes in "Revealment and Concealment in Language": "If we were to strip all the words and systems completely bare to their innermost core, in the end, after the last reduction, we should be left with nothing in our hands but one all-inclusive word. Which? Again, the same terrible 'what?' behind which stands the same 'X,' even more terrible—the nothingness.... Therefore ... the masters of poetry are forced to flee all that is fixed and inert in language, all that is opposed to their goal of the vital and mobile in language. On the contrary, using their unique keys, they are obliged to introduce into language—at every opportunity—never-ending motion, new combinations and associations.... The profane turns sacred, the sacred profane.... Meanwhile, between concealments the void looms. And that is the secret of the great influence of the language of poetry" (p. 21).

The parallels to Kafka's "Before the Law" are also conspicuous here; that story too was published at the beginning of 1915, in the independent German-Jewish weekly *Selbstwehr.*

Poems for Children (1922–1934)

The creation of a natural literature: Miron et al., *Collected Poems,* vol. III (2000), p. 153.

Bialik was well aware of the oddness and even absurdity of writing poems for children in a language that is not—or *wasn't yet*—their mother tongue (or his own). But he was also keenly aware of the importance of creating a primary register of Hebrew for a culture in the process of giving birth to itself. In that sense, as Ariel Hirschfeld has put it, Bialik was the "inventor of childhood in Hebrew" (interview in *Bialik: King of the Jews*; see also "Bialik—The Idea of Childhood and the Eros of the Poem," 2010, especially pp. 48–49). While Bialik was sometimes dismissive of this part of his oeuvre, the case has been strongly made that the poems for children "contain the hidden spiritual etymon of his work," as Ziva Shamir has written, and that he was often more open about his deepest concerns in this "lesser" genre than he was in his canonical poetry.

In a short statement about the creation of a children's literature, on the occasion of the 1922 founding in Berlin of the imprint that would be dedicated to the publication of children's books in Hebrew, he wrote: "Instead of absolute naturalness...absolute art, art which has the power to create with its charms the illusion of childhood naturalness, even in a place where it doesn't exist" (*Collected Poems*, vol. III, 2000, p. 153). Bialik wrote some eighty of these poems. Much of this work was done while he was in Germany— which is to say, after he'd extricated himself from the threats of the new Soviet Union and while he was preparing to emigrate to Palestine. There, he imagined, Hebrew-speaking children would need nursery rhymes. In fact, some of Bialik's poems for children are still

sung and read with great delight by children and parents today—
and this despite the shift from the Ashkenazic to the Sephardic
pronunciation, a transformation that allowed them to go on being
what they were: alive.

AT THE GATE (מאחורי השער)

First published in 1927. The poem seems to be rooted in an early
Yiddish adaptation of a German folk song. Readers have noted
overlaps as well with "bird poems" of Bialik's beloved Andalusian
Hebrew poetry of the eleventh and twelfth century. As with "He
Gazed and Died," we have a journey and gates; and here too the
poem is reminiscent of Kafka's "Before the Law."

THE POTTED FLOWER (עציץ פרחים)

Extant in Berlin, and first printed in Palestine, 1933. Like "See-Saw,"
the poem embodies a child's-eye view of the quintessential Biali-
kian tension between dual dimensions of experience—in this case
inside and outside, domestic and wild, artificial and natural. Cf.
"Alone" (p. 27) as a canonical poem that takes up a similar dynamic,
and of course the landmark 1916 essay "Halakhah and Aggadah."

SONG OF THE BIRDS IN THE WOODS (שירת הציפורים ביער)

Poet, translator, and children's book writer Avraham Regelson
(1896–1981) reports that Bialik once said to him: "The song of birds
in the morning is a prayer." Regelson understands that song as a
call for life and to life, and also notes parallel passages in the *Zohar.
Terumah* 130b (where the birds are angels reciting verses from
Psalms) and Yiddish folklore (on which this poem seems to be
based). Others have called this part-folksong, part-liturgical poem,
or a didactic poem for children at religious school. The date of com-
position isn't known, but the poem was extant already during the
poet's time in Berlin and was first published in 1925.

FLOWER TO BUTTERFLY (פרח לפרפר)

Date unknown; published in Palestine, 1925. There is also a com-
panion poem to this, "Butterfly to Flower" (not translated here).

THAT BIRD HAS A NEST (קן ציפור)

Extant in Berlin; first printed in 1926, in Tel Aviv. See "The Pool" for a similar Russian-doll structure worked out in one of Bialik's most accomplished canonical poems (Shamir, *Pizmonim*, pp. 36–37). A similar macrocosm-microcosm tension holds in the work of Ibn Gabirol.

ACROSS THE SEA (מעבר לים)

Date unknown. Published in 1924, Palestine. The title and the opening line fold in a marvelous shift of scale and context, with its gentle allusion to Deuteronomy 30:13: "Nor is it beyond the sea, that you should say, 'Who will go over the sea for us and bring it to us.'" That Deuteronomic overtone ripples through line 12 as well: "Where can we go up? Our brethren have discouraged our hearts, saying, 'The people *are* greater and taller than we; the cities *are* great and fortified up to heaven; moreover, we have seen the sons of the giants there'" (1:28). And finally, lines 13–16 involve marvelous shifts of context and scale, as they bring in overtones of Job 1:1, "There was a man in the land of Uz, whose name was Job; and that man was blameless and upright," and as they take us back to Deuteronomy 34:10: "But since then there has not arisen in Israel a prophet like Moses."

SEE-SAW (נדנדה)

Arguably Bialik's most famous children's poem, and one that has been called "the secret heart of [his] poetry." The date of this poem is unknown, though a version of part of it appeared, unattributed, in a children's primer published in 1906 (and subsequently reprinted many times). That collection contained several poems that we know to be by Bialik. "See-Saw" was published in full only in 1933, in Tel Aviv. Zali Gurevitch sees this as one of the poet's poems for children that "touches on the world of the adult, reading like [a] delicate haiku whose bare-bones form [is] on the verge of emptying itself of all content" (*Revealment and Concealment*, 2000, afterword, pp. 138–39). For all of its innocence, however, the poem, like the protagonist in "He Gazed and Died," hovers directly over the deepest and, according to Jewish tradition, most dangerous and in fact forbidden questions: "Whoever looks at four things is not fit to have come into the world: What is up and what is down; what is in front and what is behind" (*Hagigah* 11b). Gurevitch writes: "In its measure, weight, and lightness, [the poem itself] succeeds in simultaneously lightening the load and burdening the lightness. The poem becomes a seesaw and thus preserves the [tension between] above and below, absence and presence, self and other. The riddle remains unsolved, the lost is not quite found, and yet it is in the movement of the poem—in the revealment and concealment's domain of play, where lightness is no less important than weight—that the tension of Bialik's twofold thinking achieves its miraculous synthesis."